Gourmet's CAKES, PIES, AND COOKIES

Gourmet's CAKES, PIES, AND COOKIES

Excerpted from *Gourmet's Best Desserts*
From the Editors of *Gourmet*

CONDÉ NAST BOOKS • NEW YORK

Excerpted from *Gourmet's Best Desserts*.

Most of the recipes in this book were previously published in *Gourmet*.

Manufactured in the United States of America

98765432   24689753   23456789

Book design: Barbara Marks
Instructional illustrations: Lauren Jarrett
Decorative illustrations: Patti Hefner

PROJECT STAFF

For Condé Nast Books
Jill Cohen, Director
Jonathan E. Newhouse, Special Consultant
Ellen Maria Bruzelius, Project Manager
Kristine Smith, Project Assistant
Judith Tropea, Editorial Assistant
Diane Pesce, Composition Manager
Serafino J. Cambareri, Quality Control Manager

For *Gourmet*
Jane Montant, Editor-in-Chief
Evie Righter, Editor
Kathleen Nilon, Assistant Editor
Romulo Yanes, Staff Photographer

Produced in association with Media Projects, Incorporated.
Carter Smith, Executive Editor
Judy Knipe, Project Editor
Barbara Marks, Art Director

Gourmet Books is indebted to Georgia Chan Downard for her superb professionalism and invaluable culinary knowledge in creating and testing recipes for this project.

Gourmet Books would like to thank Zanne E. Zakroff, Kemp M. Minifie and Sara Moulton, in particular, as well as the food department of *Gourmet* for their generous participation. Appreciation is due, too, to Marjorie H. Webb and Nancy Purdum for their meticulous attention to detail in the styling of *Gourmet* photographs.

This collection would be a significantly different title were it not for the wonderful contributions of Luis Lemus, staff photographer from 1969 to 1984, and our current staff photographer, Romulo Yanes.

The text of this book was set in Bembo by the Composition Department of Condé Nast Publications, Inc. The four-color separations were done by The Color Company. The book was printed and bound by R. R. Donnelley & Sons.

CONTENTS

INTRODUCTION

Gourmet's Cakes, Pies, and Cookies is a wonderful collection of recipes selected from *Gourmet's Best Desserts*, a book presenting the very best desserts from the past twenty-five years of *Gourmet*. The recipes in this excerpted version have been chosen because of their particular suitability with the robust flavor of coffee.

To say that there is at least one recipe for everyone is an understatement. There are the classics, traditional favorites, and more contemporary combinations. And the recipes, no matter how you wish to categorize them, are all very easy to follow. Each lists equipment that is needed, and many of the recipes are preceded by helpful notes explaining some aspect or perhaps the history of the combination.

Americans have always embraced tradition, and one of them is certainly the warm and hospitable custom of the "coffee break." In many cultures coffee is part of the daily life, and the ceremony of its presentation and service often holds great importance. In the Middle East, for instance, good coffee is a distinguishing mark of hospitality; in Vienna, coffeehouses are a way of life. In Germany, and in the United States, too, a *kaffeeklatsch* refers to an enjoyable, relaxing time over coffee. "Stay for a cup of coffee" is always a welcome invitation because it promises not just coffee and good company, but perhaps a luscious dessert as well.

Gourmet's Cakes, Pies, and Cookies, with its magnificent four-color photography, represents the best of these dessert categories. We should add here that there are other wondrous desserts, equally compatible with a cup or two of coffee, that appear in the original collection.

Whether you are making the splendid recipes in this book or simply reading them for their intrinsic goodness, we hope you will enjoy this volume, a tasting from *Gourmet's Best Desserts*.

CAKES

W e celebrate with cake—birthdays, weddings, christenings, holidays. There is hardly an important event in our lives that goes unnoticed—without cake, we mean. And for good reason: Cake is a glorious concept.

To begin with, think of the number of different types of cake that exist, just awaiting delectation. There are spongecakes that can be filled and rolled or layered and iced. There are pound cakes, and loaf cakes, and Bundt cakes, and cheesecakes. There are two-layer cakes, three-layer cakes, seven-layer cakes, and tortes. There are fruitcakes and keeping cakes and cakes with fresh fruit. And those are just *some* of the types. Then there are the flavors. A chocolate cake is not a spice cake is not a vanilla cake is not a buttermilk cake. But then again, a chocolate cake is not a cocoa cake either. It is fair to say, when you come right down to it, no two cakes are alike.

Another aspect of the universal appeal of cakes has to do with the fact that no matter your level of expertise there is a cake for you to bake. Easiest to do are those one-bowl batters. Then there are the constructs—layer upon layer, with syrups and cream, and pale pink flowers on the top. You will reserve perhaps two days for that cake and regret not one minute.

History and culture are also part of cake-making. The great cuisines of the world—French, Italian, Austrian, and American—have all contributed to the repertoire. How a French cake differs from an Austrian cake is an interesting lesson in geography and government combined.

In the forty or so recipes that ensue we included numerous classic receipts, those that have stood the test of time—Dobostorte and strawberry shortcakes, as examples. We have also included some nonclassics, but wonderful combinations nonetheless. To maximize cake-making in general, information and illustrations follow on technique.

The natural sequence of events is to celebrate with cake. Let us instead celebrate the cake.

aking a cake involves three separate but equally important processes: (1) preparation of the cake batter, (2) baking of that batter and cooling of the cake, and, (3) its decorating, or finishing. Without steps 1 and 2, there is no step 3, and without a reasonably executed step 3, steps 1 and 2 are sadly compromised. In truth, a glorious cake—and there are so many wonderful recipes for them—is the sum of its parts. Let us, therefore, address each of these steps individually.

PREPARING TO BAKE

Before making a batter you will want to prepare your cake pans, preheat the oven, and assemble your ingredients, probably in that order. Be sure to butter or grease your pans carefully as even the most perfectly executed batter will look woebegone if the layer won't drop easily from the pan. Also, allow your oven to preheat sufficiently. By all means rely upon an oven thermometer. And try to ascertain if there are hot spots in your oven. If so, you will need to rotate the cake pans front to back and vice versa once during baking to ensure an even bake. Unless otherwise indicated, most cakes bake on the middle rack of the oven and that rack should be in place before you start preheating the oven.

For baking in general, but especially for the baking of cakes and pastries, it is important to measure the ingredients accurately. There is no such thing as "a touch of this and a little of that" in baking. The chemistry of cake-making does not allow for it. Therefore, the proper measuring cups are needed, particularly for the dry ingredients. Metal or plastic nested cups tend to work best, and *Gourmet* has traditionally spooned flour into the cup and leveled off the top of the cup with a spatula or knife. Know that it is this manner of measuring flour that has been used throughout in the recipes in this book. To deviate from it is to alter the amount of flour called for. Remember, too, that certain ingredients, such as baking powder, lose their potency with time and should be periodically replaced on the shelf. Now you are ready to make the batter.

MAKING THE CAKE

While cake batters differ in specific ingredients, all batters have some things in common: butter, shortening or vegetable oil, eggs, sugar, flour, and flavorings. It is the proportion of these ingredients that determines the kind of batter and, consequently, the kind of cake you make. For example, we all know that a *génoise* layer does not resemble a pound cake in texture. We also recognize that an angel food cake and a chiffon cake are not the same. We also rightfully suspect that spongecake batters differ. What differentiates each of these is its batter, and it is the ingredients of that batter and how they are combined that will render the unique characteristics of that kind of cake.

There are three different types of cakes. There are those cakes that incorporate significantly little fat and rely on beaten eggs for leavening. We call these spongecakes. Among this grouping is the renowned *génoise*, base to many a glorious combination. How this type of cake is prepared is specific and for purposes of identification will be called the sponge, or foam, method.

On the other hand, there are those that have a high fat content, meaning they rely on butter mixed most frequently with sugar, with eggs, flavorings, and flour added. These cakes are rich and moist and require a certain method of preparation to achieve that crumb. Let us call it the creaming method.

Lastly, there are those cakes that do not rely on either the sponge or creaming method, but on an ingredient that is added to bring elevation about—baking powder or baking soda or both. These are called blended batters, and they are much easier to prepare than the two kinds of batter described above.

Because *génoise* layers are so multipurpose and can be employed as the base of so many combinations—see Cassata (page 20), for example, Hazelnut Génoise with Coffee Buttercream (page 17), and even petits fours, to name just a few—it is important to know what to look for when combining this batter of eggs, sugar, flour, salt, vanilla, and clarified butter. As mentioned, it is a foam batter dependent upon beaten eggs for leavening. You begin by combining the eggs with the sugar; you then place that bowl over a pan of simmering water and stir the mixture until warm and the sugar is thoroughly dissolved (see illustration page 10). Do not allow the bottom of the bowl to touch the hot water. It is primarily the combination of the heat and the stirring that expands the molecules in the eggs. You then remove the bowl from the pan and with an electric mixer beat the batter until it triples in volume. This is a very clear point in the stage of this batter and the signal to proceed with quickly folding in the dry ingredients, and lastly, the clarified butter. A *génoise* batter should then be poured into the prepared pan(s) and baked immediately.

For other foam method cakes, the batter is actually beaten with an electric mixer to a point where it falls in a ribbon back on itself (see illustra-

Beating over simmering water

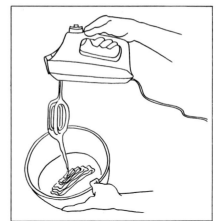

Falling in a ribbon

tion above). This is yet another way of incorporating as much air as possible into the batter, which in turn leavens the cake.

As specific as the preparation of a foam batter is, so is preparation of a creamed batter. You begin by beating air into softened butter and sugar and you continue to work air into that batter until it has achieved a creamy, full texture. When that batter has achieved that texture, it is ready to be baked, and, unless your eyes were deceiving you, you can expect a strong, healthy elevation from such a correctly air-filled prepared batter.

Blended batters are by far and away the easiest ones to combine and, as already noted, depend upon no specific stage of preparation for leavening. Baking powder and baking soda or both, and even yeast, will provide the chemical impetus.

With the batter made, you can proceed to the truly fascinating aspect of cake-baking, the transformation of batter that occurs in combination with heat.

BAKING THE CAKE

While some culinary combinations lend themselves to being made in advance, cake batters do not fall into this convenient category. Once made, a batter, especially one with baking powder or stiffly beaten egg whites, for that matter, should be baked.

As mentioned earlier, unless otherwise indicated, cakes bake on the middle rack of a preheated oven. Know, too, that baking times are not written in stone. They are indications. Your oven, or an environmental factor like altitude, will have a sizable effect on how long a cake bakes. Therefore, slightly before the end of the suggested baking time start testing your cake for doneness. You can use a wooden skewer, a toothpick, or a clean broom straw. Some sources might suggest inserting a knife into the center of the layer, but we believe the thinner the tester the better.

It is easy to tell when a tester inserted into a cake comes out "clean" or "with crumbs adhering to it." It is also obvious when the tester comes out wet—with batter on it—as is sometimes desired. In this specific instance, though, it is not necessarily obvious that the cake is actually baked through. Here is where the suggested time for a cake to remain in the pan on a rack becomes significant. During that period a cake continues to cook, and in its own way, set. We've all had experiences when, in a rush, we tried to unmold a cake almost straight from the oven. Without having had the opportunity to finish baking, or to cool and contract, as the case may be, the layer is far too fragile, to say nothing of hot, to unmold.

When the cake is ready to unmold, using one hand, bring the cooling rack right up to the rim of the cake pan, which you hold in your other hand with your palm stretched out along the bottom. Gently turn the cake pan upside down on the rack. To dump a cake is a most successful way of breaking it.

As important as it is to let a cake cool in the pan on a rack, allowing air to fully circulate, so it is important to let the cake cool completely out of the pan. Recognize, though, that certain cakes, if left to cool for too long, can develop a hard crust. You do not want to leave any cake to cool on the counter overnight.

FINISHING THE CAKE

With a cooled cake you can proceed to finishing it, or to putting the icing on the cake! This might be as simple as sifting confectioners' sugar on top, as we do with Sand Torte (page 48), or having a sugar or chocolate glaze ready and pouring it over the top of the cake. See Scripture Cake (page 49) and Armagnac Chocolate Cake with Prunes (page 43). And then again, it might mean pulling out the stops as we do with Chocolate Raspberry Dobostorte (page 66), where a buttercream and caramel adorn the glorious finished product. Needless to say, experience and nerve dictate the cakes one bakes and decorates.

Regardless of your level of experience, cake decorating requires practice. No one, not even the most adroit baker, has learned how to work a pastry bag overnight. Decorating cakes also necessitates equipment:
- several light-weight pastry bags with an assortment of decorative tips, which would initially include a plain, star, and fluted tip
- a cake stand
- a cake comb
- a collection of different sized spatulas

All of these will be available at better kitchenware stores.
More than anything else, though, you will need time and the opportunity
to practice. Think of the splendid reasons you now have for baking cakes!

Let us assume you are decorating a layer cake such as Hazelnut Génoise with Coffee Buttercream (page 17). You will have made your buttercream while the cake is cooling. Your layers are now on the counter; your
equipment is assembled. You begin by slicing the cakes into layers. As illustrated opposite, place one hand on the top of one of the layers to gently
anchor it. Then, using a long-bladed, serrated knife, cut the cake horizontally through the center into even layers. There is no reason to rotate the
cake; with a simple sawing motion cut it apart. Transfer the bottom layer
to a cake stand, if you are using one, and spread the cut side of it evenly
with buttercream or another filling of choice—jam, for instance. Replace
the top layer, cut side down, on top of the filling. Split, fill, and stack the
remaining layer in the same manner.

There are several ways to position a cake to make it easier to apply
the frosting. As shown on page 13, you can hold the cake in one hand on
your outstretched palm. You can also place the cake on an inverted cake
pan of the same size as the cake. Or you can place it on a cake stand. It is
easier to frost a cake if the sides are free-standing, and in this regard we
highly recommend a turntable, available at better kitchenware stores, if
you are eager for a professionally finished appearance to your cake. If you
opt to frost the cake on the platter on which you are going to serve it, cover
the edge of the platter with strips of wax paper, which you can simply remove by pulling gently from under the cake when you have finished
decorating it.

Using an appropriately sized spatula, spread the sides of the cake
first, using a flicking downward motion of your wrist, and then the top
evenly with buttercream. To achieve a very smooth final finish, then hold
the spatula stationary in one hand against the buttercream on the sides of
the cake and rotate the cake to even out the icing. This is a simultaneous
action and a very consistent amount of gentle pressure should be applied
to the spatula, otherwise the buttercream on one side of the cake will be
thicker than on the other. To level out the buttercream on the top of the
cake, lay the spatula flat against the buttercream and rotate the cake as before. When you are done, you should have a beautiful smooth surface that
doesn't even suggest use of a spatula. Practice will make this easier to do as
well.

You are now ready to finish the cake. The choice of how you want to
do this is yours, despite what a recipe might dictate. There is the cake
comb which, when drawn around the top or sides of the cake, renders a
very, simple pretty, circular ridged pattern. It is also easy and fast to do.
Press some toasted chopped nuts around the sides of the cake, and *c'est fini*,
the cake is finished.

For a more elaborate presentation, you can decorate the cake with
rosettes of buttercream, just one of many designs you will come to recog-

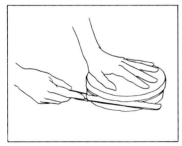
Slicing horizontally

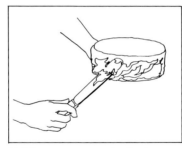
Holding on outstretched palm

Positioning on cake pan

Positioning on cake stand

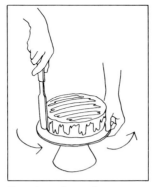
Rotating cake to frost

Using cake comb

nize. This will involve working with the pastry bag. You will first need to select the proper tip, a selection of which is shown in the illustrations on page 14. Each tip produces a different design, as you can tell from the names. The more proficient you become with a pastry bag, the larger your collection of decorative tips will grow.

To make rosettes you will be using a star, also known as a rosette, tip. Fit it onto the pastry bag; then using the spatula to transfer buttercream, fill the bag as shown on page 14. Use a manageable amount of buttercream to begin with. Twist the top of the bag closed and at the same time gently squeeze the buttercream in the bag down toward the tip. You are now ready to start forming rosettes, or swirls. Holding the top of the bag in one hand, put your other hand at the bottom near the tip and guide the bag in a circular motion, or spiral, as you gently apply pressure on the buttercream to extrude it onto the top of the cake. Finish the spiral by lifting the tip straight up and continue making rosettes in the same manner. The key to making rosettes, or any pattern, lies in the amount of pressure you use on the bag.

Should you want to finish the rosettes with, let us say, a touch of chocolate glaze or a different-colored buttercream, there is no need to utilize another pastry bag. Using parchment or wax paper you can form a cone that acts as a pastry bag. This improvisation is put to good use in bakeries and pastry shops, where each color of frosting requires yet another

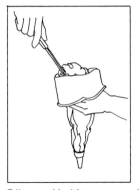   

Filling and holding a pastry bag

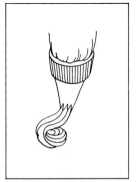  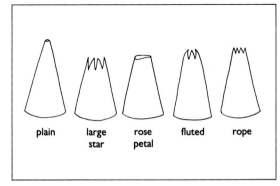

Piping a rosette

plain   large
star   rose
petal   fluted   rope

Assorted pastry tips

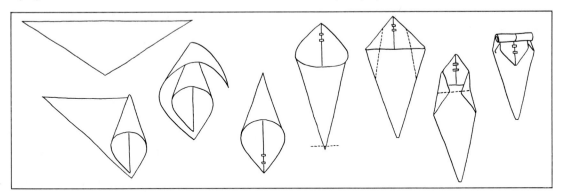

Forming a parchment paper cone

 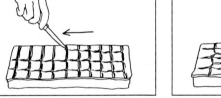 

Feathering icing

clean pastry bag. You will find this paper cone comes in very handy when decorating Gingerbread Men (page 157) with Sugar Icing (page 172). Following the illustrations opposite, simply cut a triangle of paper, form it into a tight cone, and fill it with a small amount of frosting.

Fine finishing also includes a technique called feathering, which requires no special equipment once you have applied the frosting that you are going to detail. As shown in the illustration opposite, gently draw a knife through the icing, pulling it in one direction, creating a feathery, fluted effect. Then pull the knife in the opposite direction. The pattern looks far more complicated than its execution dictates.

This short primer on cake decorating only hints at the wonders that can be created with frosting and a pastry bag. When you are up for a challenge, attempt other marvelous devices, like Marzipan Decorations (page 170), that amuse the top of Carrot Cake with Cream Cheese Frosting (page 37).

With a cake the pleasures are endless. There is the fun of making and decorating it, and then the joy of eating it. No sooner is that done than the next cake calls.

GÉNOISE

We know *génoise* layers as those extraordinarily light French cakes made of eggs, sugar, flour, and clarified butter. In fact, the history books have it that *génoise*, as its name indicates, originated in Genoa, Italy, then traveled to France, where it found a permanent home.

What we also know about *génoise* is that it is not a simple batter. It needs to be beaten with an electric mixer to three times its original volume; in short, while you might contemplate trying to do something like this by hand, you are advised not to. But do not avoid making *génoise* on account of this. The cake acts as the foundation of any number of wonderful desserts. It is eminently adaptable and lends itself to being layered not only with buttercream but also with ice cream, and *crème anglaise*, and even pastry cream.

There is vanilla *génoise*, chocolate *génoise*. There are *génoise* layers and sheets. *Génoise* rolls, *génoise* slices. If you want to master one very basic batter, which *Gourmet* has relied upon for years with great success, *génoise* is the one to conquer. (For information on the combining of the batter and an illustration, see pages 9 and 10.)

VANILLA GÉNOISE BATTER

Yield:
two 9-inch layers

Equipment:
hand-held electric
  mixer

6 large eggs
1 cup sugar
1 cup all-purpose flour
¾ teaspoon salt

1½ teaspoons vanilla
6 tablespoons clarified butter (page
  164), melted and cooled to
  lukewarm

In a metal bowl whisk together the eggs and the sugar, set the bowl over a pan of simmering water, and stir the mixture until warm and the sugar is dissolved (see illustration page 10). Remove the bowl from the pan and with the mixer beat the mixture at moderate speed for 10 to 15 minutes, or until it is triple in volume and cooled to room temperature. While the eggs are being beaten, sift the flour with the salt onto a sheet of wax paper and in a bowl combine the vanilla and the clarified butter. Sift and fold the flour mixture in batches into the egg mixture until the mixture is just combined, stir one fourth of the mixture into the butter mixture, and fold the butter mixture quickly into the batter.

Variation:

CHOCOLATE GÉNOISE BATTER: Reduce the amount of flour to ⅔ cup and add ⅓ cup unsweetened cocoa powder. Sift the flour and cocoa, one third at a time, into the beaten egg mixture. Proceed with the recipe as directed.

GÉNOISE SHEET CAKE

Yield:
one 15½ by 10½
  inches sheet

Equipment:
jelly-roll pan, 15½ by
  10½ inches

1 recipe vanilla or chocolate génoise batter (recipe above)

Butter the jelly-roll pan, line it with wax paper, leaving a 2-inch overhang on both short ends, and butter the paper. Preheat the oven to 350° F.
   Pour the *génoise* batter into the pan, spreading it evenly with a metal spatula. Bake the sheet in the middle of the oven for 20 minutes, or until the paper pulls away easily from the ends of the cake. Cover the cake with wax paper and a baking sheet, and invert the cake onto the baking sheet. Peel off the wax paper and trim away any rough edges from the sides of the cake. Cover the cake with a fresh piece of wax paper, roll it up, and let the cake cool completely.
   Unroll, fill, and reroll the cake. Transfer the cake carefully with metal spatulas to a cake board.

HAZELNUT GÉNOISE WITH COFFEE BUTTERCREAM

Yield:
one 8-inch cake

Equipment:
two 8-inch cake pans
upright electric mixer
pastry brush
candy thermometer
7-inch cardboard
   round

1 recipe vanilla génoise *batter (recipe opposite)*

FOR THE COFFEE BUTTERCREAM

6 egg yolks
¾ cup sugar
⅓ cup water
2½ sticks (1¼ cups) unsalted butter,
*   softened*

2 tablespoons coffee extract, or to
*   taste, made by mixing 2*
*   tablespoons instant freeze-dried*
*   coffee or espresso with 1 tablespoon*
*   boiling water*
1 to 2 tablespoons Cognac or rum

½ recipe sugar syrup (page 166) with
*   1 to 2 tablespoons Cognac or rum*
*   added when syrup cools to room*
*   temperature*

1 cup finely ground hazelnut praline
*   (page 167)*

Butter the cake pans, line the bottoms with wax paper, and butter the paper. Dust the pans with flour, knocking out the excess. Preheat the oven to 350° F.

Pour the *génoise* batter into the pans, smoothing the tops, and bake the layers in the middle of the oven for 20 to 25 minutes, or until the tops are golden and a tester comes out clean. Let the layers cool in the pans on a rack for 5 minutes, invert the cakes onto racks, and carefully remove the wax paper. Let the cakes cool completely.

Make the buttercream:

In the bowl of the mixer beat the egg yolks until light and thick. In a small heavy saucepan combine the sugar and the water. Bring the syrup to a boil and boil it over moderate heat, stirring and washing down any sugar crystals clinging to the sides of the pan with the brush dipped in cold water until it reaches the soft-ball stage, or the candy thermometer registers 238° F.

With the mixer running, pour the hot syrup into the yolks in a stream, beating, and continue to beat the mixture until it is completely cool. Beat in the butter, a little at a time, add coffee extract to taste, and beat well. Stir in the Cognac or rum. Chill the coffee buttercream, covered, until firm but still soft enough to spread.

The layers may be made up to 1 day in advance and kept wrapped in plastic wrap at room temperature. The cake may be assembled up to 2 days in advance, covered loosely with plastic wrap, and chilled. Let the cake come to room temperature before serving.

Put 1 teaspoon of the buttercream in the center of the cardboard round. Halve one of the layers horizontally with a serrated knife, arrange one half-layer, cut side up, on the cardboard round, and brush some of the sugar syrup over the cake. Cover the layer with a ¼-inch-thick layer of buttercream, smoothing it with a metal spatula, and sprinkle it with 2 tablespoons of the hazelnut praline.

Set the second half-layer, bottom side up, on the buttercream, pressing down slightly, and moisten the top of the cake with sugar syrup. Cover the top with a ¼-inch-thick layer of buttercream, smoothing it with a metal spatula, and sprinkle it with 2 tablespoons of the hazelnut praline.

Halve the remaining cake horizontally and continue to layer the cake, ending with a fourth layer, bottom side up. Moisten the top of the cake with sugar syrup and cover the sides and top with the remaining buttercream, smoothing it with the spatula. Press the remaining hazelnut praline around the sides of the cake and chill the *génoise* until the buttercream is set.

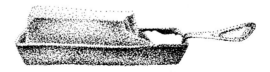

GÉNOISE WITH KIRSCH FONDANT AND FRESH STRAWBERRIES

Yield:
one 7½-inch cake

Enchanting to look at, this fluted *génoise* is iced with shiny fondant and decorated with fondant-dipped strawberries. A cake for an occasion.

Equipment:
7½-inch fluted cake pan or *Kugelhupf* mold
candy thermometer

½ recipe vanilla génoise *batter (page 16)*
2 recipes fondant (page 165)

¼ cup kirsch
3 or 4 drops red food coloring

20 large unblemished strawberries, with hulls on, for garnish

Butter the fluted cake pan well and preheat the oven to 350° F.

Pour the *génoise* batter into the prepared pan and bake the cake in the middle of the oven for 30 minutes, or until it is puffed and golden and pulls away easily from the sides of the pan. Turn the *génoise* out onto a rack and let it cool completely.

Place the fondant in the top of a double boiler and let it soften over hot water. Stir in the kirsch and the food coloring. Do not let the fondant become too hot or it will lose its shine. Should the fondant become too thick, thin it with a little unbeaten egg white or with small amount of sugar syrup (page 166) cooked until the candy thermometer registers 220° F.

To assemble the cake:
Line a jelly-roll pan with wax paper, set a rack on top of it, and place the *génoise* on the rack. Pour the fondant over the cake, letting it drip down the sides, leaving a smooth, thin coating. Transfer the cake to a serving plate.

With a metal spatula scrape up the fondant from the jelly-roll pan and put it in a small saucepan. Melt the fondant over very low heat and dip the tips of the strawberries into it, letting the excess run off. Lay the berries on a sheet of wax paper and let the fondant dry. Garnish the top of the cake and the serving plate, if desired, with the berries.

CREOLE CHEESE GÂTEAU

Yield:
one 6-inch cake

Equipment:
jelly-roll pan, 17¾ by
11¾ by 1½ inches
upright electric mixer
6-inch springform
pan, 3 inches deep
parchment paper
6-inch cake pan
pastry brush
pastry bag fitted with
fluted tip

1 recipe vanilla génoise batter (page 16)

FOR THE CREOLE CHEESE
1 teaspoon unflavored gelatin
3 tablespoons cold water
1¼ cups well-chilled heavy cream
4 ounces cream cheese, well softened

⅓ cup superfine granulated sugar
1 teaspoon grated lemon rind
1 teaspoon vanilla

1 recipe brandy syrup (page 166)
*1 cup seedless raspberry jam, melted
    and cooled*

12 large whole strawberries
2 cups sweetened whipped cream

Line the jelly-roll pan with wax paper and butter the paper. Preheat the oven to 350° F.

Pour the *génoise* batter into the jelly-roll pan, spreading it evenly with a spatula, and bake the cake in the middle of the oven for 20 minutes, or until lightly browned. Loosen the wax paper from the sides of the pan and invert the sponge sheet onto a baking sheet. Let the cake cool and peel off the paper.

Make the Creole cheese:

In a small bowl sprinkle the gelatin over the water and let it soften for 10 minutes. Set the bowl over simmering water and stir the gelatin until dissolved. Let cool. In a chilled bowl with the mixer beat the heavy cream until it holds soft peaks. In a large bowl combine the cream cheese, sugar, lemon rind, and vanilla. Stir in the cooled gelatin mixture and fold in the whipped cream.

To assemble the cake:

Line the bottom and sides of the springform pan with the parchment paper and extend the sides by tying a strip of parchment paper around the pan to form a collar. Using the 6-inch cake pan as a guide, cut 2 rounds from the sponge sheet, reserving the remaining cake for another use. Moisten one side of the sponge layers with the brandy syrup and fit one layer into the springform pan. Spread a thin layer of the raspberry jam on the sponge and top it with a ¾-inch layer of the Creole cheese. Top the cheese with the remaining sponge layer, moistened side down, and brush the top with the syrup. Fill the pan with the remaining Creole cheese. Chill the cake for at least 4 hours or overnight.

Remove the sides of the pan, remove the parchment paper, and transfer the cake to a cake stand. Spread a thin layer of jam in the center of the cake, then arrange decoratively several strawberries in the middle of the jam. Brush the berries with jam, pipe rosettes of whipped cream around the top of the cake, and chill the cake until ready to serve.

CASSATA

Ricotta and Ice-Cream Cake

Yield:
one 8- by 4-inch loaf
cake

This renowned Italian ice-cream cake has layers of *génoise* separated by ricotta filling and strawberry ice cream. While vanilla cake is the classic preparation, a chocolate sheet cake would make a lovely variation.

Equipment:
food processor fitted
with steel blade
loaf pan, 8 by 4 by 4
inches
hand-held electric
mixer
pastry bag fitted with
large star tip

1 vanilla génoise *sheet cake (page 16), cooled but not rolled*

FOR THE FILLING
1 pound ricotta
¼ cup superfine granulated sugar
¼ cup heavy cream

¼ cup orange-flavored liqueur
¼ cup chopped glacéed mixed fruits
2 ounces semisweet chocolate, chopped

2 pints strawberry ice cream, softened
1½ cups well-chilled heavy cream
¼ cup confectioners' sugar, sifted

¼ cup orange-flavored liqueur
chopped glacéed fruits for garnish

Make the filling:

In the food processor combine the ricotta, the sugar, cream, and orange-flavored liqueur. Transfer the mixture to a bowl and fold in the glacéed fruits and the chocolate. Chill, covered, for 2 hours, or until the filling is firm, but still of spreading consistency.

Line the loaf pan with plastic wrap. Cut the *génoise* sheet crosswise into four 8- by 4-inch strips and fit one of the strips into the bottom of the loaf pan. Spread 1 pint of the strawberry ice cream over the cake and freeze the dessert for 30 minutes, or until the ice cream is firm.

Top the ice cream with a second layer of sponge sheet, pressing it down slightly, and spread the ricotta cheese filling over the cake. Top the filling with a third layer of sponge sheet, pressing it down slightly. Spread the remaining 1 pint strawberry ice cream over it and chill the layers until the ice cream is firm. Top the dessert with another layer of sponge sheet (the cake need not be in one piece), and chill the cake, covered with plastic wrap, for 30 minutes, or until the ice cream is firm. Weight the cake lightly and freeze it overnight.

In a chilled bowl with the mixer beat the heavy cream with the confectioners' sugar and the orange-flavored liqueur until it holds soft peaks. Release the cake from the sides of the pan with a knife, invert it onto a chilled platter, and remove the plastic wrap. Spread the whipped cream smoothly over the sides and top of the cake with a spatula, reserving a small amount of it. Put the reserved whipped cream into the pastry bag and pipe it decoratively over the cake. Arrange the chopped glacéed fruits over the cream. Chill the cake for 2 hours before serving. To serve, cut the cake in thin slices.

Photo on page 97.

ORANGE GÉNOISE WITH ORANGE BUTTERCREAM

Yield:
one 9-inch cake

Equipment:
two 9-inch round
 cake pans, 1½
 inches deep
upright electric mixer
pastry brush
candy thermometer

Here is the classic *génoise* combination. Two light layers are brushed with flavored syrup, then the whole is iced with buttercream and fancifully decorated. A splendid cake for the summer.

1 recipe vanilla génoise batter (page 16)

FOR THE ORANGE BUTTERCREAM

6 egg yolks
¾ cup sugar
⅓ cup water
2 or 3 drops yellow food coloring
2 or 3 drops red food coloring
2½ sticks (1¼ cups) unsalted butter,
 very well softened

¼ cup orange-flavored liqueur
½ drop red food coloring
½ drop yellow food coloring

FOR THE SYRUP

½ cup sugar
½ cup water

¼ cup orange-flavored liqueur

the rind of 3 navel oranges, cut into
 ¾-inch julienne strips and blanched
 in boiling water for 5 minutes

1 recipe apricot glaze (page 165) with
 2 to 3 tablespoons orange-flavored
 liqueur added

thin slices of navel orange, peeled, for garnish

Butter the cake pans, sprinkle them with flour, and knock out the excess. Preheat the oven to 350° F.

Pour the *génoise* batter into the the cake pans and bake in the middle of the oven for 20 to 25 minutes, or until golden. Invert the layers onto a rack and let them cool completely.

Make the orange buttercream:
In the bowl of the mixer beat the egg yolks until light and thick. In a small heavy saucepan combine the sugar and water. Bring the syrup to a boil and boil it over moderate heat, stirring and washing down any sugar crystals clinging to the pan with the brush dipped in cold water until it reaches the soft-ball stage, or the candy thermometer registers 238° F.

With the mixer running, pour the hot syrup into the yolks in a stream, beating, and continue to beat the mixture until it is completely cool. Beat in the butter, one tablespoon at a time, add the liqueur, and beat well. Stir in the food coloring. Chill the buttercream, covered, until firm, but still soft enough to spread.

Make the syrup:
In a small heavy saucepan dissolve the sugar in the water over moderate heat and cook for 5 minutes. Remove the pan from the heat and stir in the liqueur.

Refresh the strips of orange rind under running cold water and pat them dry with paper towels. In a bowl combine them with the apricot glaze.

To assemble the cake: Invert one of the 9-inch cake pans and put 1 teaspoon of the orange buttercream in the center of the tin. Set a *génoise* layer on the tin and brush the top with syrup. Cover the layer with a ¼-inch-thick layer of the buttercream, smoothing it with a metal spatula. Chill the cake for 10 to 15 minutes, or until the buttercream is quite firm. Set the second *génoise* layer, bottom side up, on the buttercream, pressing down slightly, and moisten the top of the cake with orange-liqueur syrup. Cover the top and sides with the remaining buttercream, smoothing it with the spatula. Press the glazed strips of orange julienne onto the sides of the cake. Decorate the top with the peeled orange slices and brush the slices with some of the glaze. Arrange bunches of glazed strips of orange julienne in the center of each orange slice. Chill the cake until the buttercream is firm.

Photo on page 98.

TORTES

Some people associate the word *torte* with a cake made of ground nuts, and they are not wrong. The definition of *torte*, however, also includes a cake of either German or Austrian descent that is layered with fillings or icings, jams, or whipped cream—the imporant part being that it is layered. The tortes that follow fall within this description and, as you can imagine, share layers in common, and great variety besides.

Two of the three tortes that follow derive from Austria, land of sophisticated *Konditorei* and bowls of whipped cream. Kaisertorte (page 24), imperial sounding, stands high, in three layers, and is made of and glazed with chocolate. Sugar Kirsch Torte (page 26) in true European splendor combines light *génoise* layers, meringue layers, and a delicately colored, pale pink buttercream. The remaining torte in this grouping is a glorious combination of white cake, drifty white buttercream made with only egg whites, and fresh raspberries. A perfect summer offering.

There is something Old World and wonderful about tortes. Perhaps it is because some of them, like the kirsch combination, are so lovely to look at and fanciful. Remember: Even that remarkable dessert started with a simple *génoise* layer.

RASPBERRY TORTE

Yield:
one 8-inch layer cake

1 recipe vanilla génoise batter (page 16)

Equipment:
two 8-inch round
  cake pans
pastry brush
candy thermometer
upright electric mixer
7-inch cardboard
  round

FOR THE BUTTERCREAM
1¼ cups sugar
⅓ cup water
5 egg whites at room temperature
pinch of salt
⅛ teaspoon cream of tartar

3 sticks (1½ cups) unsalted butter,
* softened*
2 to 3 tablespoons eau-de-vie de
* framboise (raspberry brandy), or*
* to taste*

FOR THE SUGAR SYRUP
⅓ cup sugar
⅓ cup water

1 tablespoon eau-de-vie de
* framboise (raspberry brandy)*

⅔ cup sieved raspberry preserves
2½ cups fresh raspberries

2 cups raspberry sauce (page 173) as
* an accompaniment*

Make the *génoise*:
Preheat the oven to 350° F. Butter the cake pans, line the bottoms with wax paper, and butter the paper. Dust the pans with flour, knocking out the excess.

Divide the *génoise* batter between the cake pans, smoothing the tops, and bake the layers in the middle of the oven for 20 to 25 minutes, or until the tops are golden and a cake tester inserted in the centers comes out clean. Let the cakes cool in the pans on a rack for 5 minutes, invert the layers onto a cake rack, remove the paper, and let the layers cool completely.

Make the buttercream:
In a small heavy saucepan combine the sugar with the water. Bring the mixture to a boil and boil it over moderate heat, stirring and washing down any sugar crystals clinging to the sides of the pan with the brush dipped in cold water until it reaches the hard-ball stage, or the candy thermometer reaches 248° F.

In the bowl of the mixer beat the egg whites with the salt until frothy. Add the cream of tartar and beat the whites until they hold stiff but not dry peaks. With the mixer running, add the hot syrup to the whites in a stream, beating, and beat the mixture until completely cool. Beat in the butter, a little at a time, and add the *framboise*. Chill the buttercream, covered, until firm but still soft enough to spread.

Make the sugar syrup:
In a small saucepan combine the sugar with the water. Bring the mixture to a boil, stirring, and simmer it until clear. Let the mixture cool to room temperature and stir in the *eau-de-vie de framboise*.

To assemble the torte:
Put 1 teaspoon of the buttercream in the center of the cardboard round. With a serrated knife halve one of the cake layers horizontally (see illustration page 13). Place one half-layer, cut side up, on the cardboard round and brush some of the syrup over it. With a spatula smooth a thin layer of the raspberry preserves over the cake. Cover the preserves with a ¼-inch-

thick layer of the buttercream, smoothing it with a spatula. Set aside 12 raspberries for the garnish and sprinkle one third of the remaining raspberries over the cake. Set the second half-layer, bottom side up, on the buttercream, pressing down slightly. Repeat layers of syrup, preserves, buttercream, and half the remaining raspberries. Halve the remaining cake layer horizontally and continue to layer the cake, ending with the last cake layer, bottom side up. Brush the top of the cake with the syrup and coat it with a thin layer of raspberry preserves. Cover the sides and top of the cake with the remaining buttercream, smoothing it with the spatula, and with the spatula or a long knife score 12 slices on the top of the torte.

Garnish the top of the torte with the reserved raspberries, transfer the torte carefully to a cake plate, and serve with the raspberry sauce.

The torte may be prepared up to 2 days in advance and kept chilled, covered loosely with plastic wrap. Let the torte come to room temperature before serving.

KAISERTORTE

Toasted Almond and Chocolate Torte

Yield:
one 8-inch cake

This Austrian specialty, with its distinctive decoration, combines chocolate almond layers, chocolate buttercream, and chocolate glaze.

Equipment:
8-inch springform pan
hand-held electric
  mixer
food processor fitted
  with steel blade
3-inch round cutter

FOR THE CAKE
2½ ounces dark sweet chocolate,
  chopped
½ stick (¼ cup) unsalted butter
5 large eggs, separated, at room
  temperature
3 tablespoons confectioners' sugar
1½ teaspoons vanilla

1½ teaspoons dark rum
1 cup whole blanched almonds (for
  procedure page 174), toasted
⅓ cup all-purpose flour
¼ teaspoon salt
¼ teaspoon cream of tartar
½ cup granulated sugar

FOR THE CHOCOLATE BUTTERCREAM
3 ounces dark sweet chocolate,
  chopped
3 sticks (1½ cups) unsalted butter,
  softened

1⅓ cups sifted confectioners' sugar
4 egg yolks
½ teaspoon vanilla

FOR THE GLAZE
1½ ounces dark sweet chocolate,
  chopped
3 ounces (⅔ cup) sugar cubes

2 tablespoons hot water
½ teaspoon flavorless vegetable oil

¾ cup sliced blanched almonds, toasted

Make the cake:

Preheat the oven to 350° F. Butter the springform pan, line the bottom with wax paper, and butter the paper. Dust the pan with flour and knock out the excess.

In the top of a double boiler set over simmering water melt the chocolate with the butter, stirring, and let the mixture cool.

In a large bowl with the mixer beat the egg yolks with the confectioners' sugar until the mixture is thick and lemon colored. Beat in the vanilla and rum. Add the melted chocolate mixture and combine well. In the food processor or in a blender grind the almonds with the flour to a powder. In a large bowl with the mixer beat the egg whites with the salt until frothy, add the cream of tartar, and beat the whites until they hold soft peaks. Add the granulated sugar, one tablespoon at a time, beating, and beat until the whites hold stiff peaks. Stir one fourth of the whites into the chocolate mixture. Fold in the remaining whites and the almond flour mixture gently but thoroughly. Spoon the batter into the springform pan, smooth the top, and bake the cake in the middle of the oven for 35 to 40 minutes, or until a cake tester inserted in the center comes out clean. Let the cake cool in the pan on a rack.

Make the chocolate buttercream: In the top of a double boiler set over simmering water melt the chocolate and let it cool. In a bowl with the mixer cream the butter. Add ⅓ cup of the confectioners' sugar and beat until light and fluffy. In another bowl with the mixer beat the egg yolks until thick and lemon colored. Gradually add the remaining 1 cup confectioners' sugar and the vanilla, beating, and beat the mixture well. Beat the butter mixture into the yolk mixture, a little at a time, and beat the mixture until smooth. Add the melted chocolate and combine the buttercream well.

Run a thin knife around the sides of the pan, remove the sides carefully, and with a serrated knife cut the cake horizontally into 3 layers (see illustration page 13). Place the bottom layer, cut side up, on a cake plate and spread it with 1 cup of the buttercream. Top with the middle cake layer. Spread the middle layer with 1 cup of the buttercream and top it with the remaining cake layer, cut side down.

Make the glaze: In the top of a double boiler set over simmering water melt the chocolate, stirring. In a small heavy saucepan combine the sugar cubes and the hot water and cook the mixture over moderately low heat, stirring, until the sugar is dissolved. Bring the glaze to a boil over moderate heat, remove the pan from the heat, and, working quickly, add the chocolate and the oil, stirring until smooth.

Pour the glaze immediately onto the center of the torte and with a knife dipped in hot water spread it into a 6-inch round. Press the cutter lightly onto the center of the glaze and leave it in place. Spread the remaining buttercream around the sides of the torte and over the top, covering the edges of the glaze but leaving the area protected by the cutter untouched. Press the sliced almonds gently onto the buttercream, covering it almost completely, and remove the cutter.

Chill the torte for at least 2 hours. Let the torte stand at room temperature for 20 minutes before serving.

SUGAR KIRSCH TORTE

Yield:
one 7-inch cake

Equipment:
7-inch round cake
  pan, 2 inches deep
upright electric mixer
pastry brush
small pastry bag fitted
  with star tip

This culinary construction of *génoise* layers, meringue layers, and pale pink buttercream is as extraordinary to look at as it is to taste.

1 recipe vanilla génoise *batter (page 16)*

FOR THE MERINGUE LAYERS
4 egg whites at room temperature
pinch of salt
1 cup sugar

½ cup blanched almonds (for procedure page 174), lightly toasted and ground

FOR THE BUTTERCREAM
4 egg yolks
1 cup sugar
½ cup milk, scalded

2½ sticks (1¼ cups) unsalted butter, softened
¼ cup kirsch
a few drops of red food coloring

FOR THE SUGAR SYRUP
¼ cup sugar
¼ cup water

¼ cup kirsch

½ cup blanched almonds, lightly toasted and chopped coarse

Preheat the oven to 350° F. Butter and lightly flour the cake pan.

Pour the *génoise* batter into the pan and bake the cake in the middle of the oven for 25 minutes, or until it is golden and shrinks from the sides of the pan. Remove the cake from the pan and let it cool on a rack.

Reduce the oven temperature to 250° F.

Make the meringue layers: In the bowl of the mixer beat the egg whites with the salt until frothy. Beat in the sugar, a little at a time, and continue beating the meringue until it is very stiff. Fold in the ground almonds.

Draw two 7-inch circles on a sheet of wax paper and lay the paper on a baking sheet. Spread the meringue ¼ inch thick within the circles and bake the layers in the middle of the oven for 45 minutes, or until hard and dry. Let the meringue layers cool on the baking sheet and carefully remove them from the paper.

Make the buttercream: In the bowl of the mixer beat the egg yolks with the sugar until light and lemon colored. Pour in the scalded milk in a thin stream, stirring. Transfer the mixture to a saucepan and cook it over low heat without letting it boil, stirring, until it is thick enough to coat a spoon. Put the saucepan in a bowl of ice water and stir the custard until barely warm. Transfer the custard to the bowl of the mixer, turn the mixer to high, and beat in the butter, one tablespoon at a time. Continue to beat the buttercream until it holds stiff peaks. Beat in the kirsch and the food coloring. Chill the buttercream until firm but still of spreading consistency.

Make the sugar syrup: In a small saucepan dissolve the sugar in the water over moderate heat and cook for 5 minutes. Remove the pan from the heat and stir in the kirsch.

To assemble the torte: Using a serrated knife, cut the *génoise* in half horizontally (see illustration page 13) and brush the cut side of each layer with the warm kirsch syrup. Put 1 teaspoon of the buttercream in the center of one of the cake pans, inverted, and set one of the meringue layers, smooth side down, on the pan. Spread a thin layer of buttercream over the meringue. Top it with one of the *génoise* layers, cut side up, and spread the cake with some of the buttercream. Cover the buttercream with the remaining *génoise* layer, cut side down, and spread the cake with more of the buttercream. Put the second meringue layer, smooth side up, on top of the buttercream. Trim the sides of the cake. With a metal spatula smooth some of the buttercream on the sides and top of the cake, reserving about ⅓ cup. Fill the pastry bag with the reserved buttercream and pipe ribbons on top of the torte. Press some of the chopped almonds around the base of the torte and sprinkle a few almonds decoratively on the top. Transfer the torte to a serving plate and chill it for 2 hours.

Photo on page 99.

SPONGECAKES AND ROLLED CAKES

Earlier in this chapter we mentioned the versatility with which sponge-cakes can be made. Some depend solely upon beaten egg whites for their leavening. Others incorporate whole eggs, first the yolks and then the beaten whites, as well as baking powder and/or baking soda for an airy, light texture. No matter the variations of components, though, the crumb of a spongecake is delicate and fine.

The batters for spongecakes lend themselves to being baked in sheet pans, or jelly-roll pans, the first step to a rolled cake. And the variety of rolled cakes is endless and exceptionally pleasing. Think of it: There are beloved jelly rolls—see our Great American Jelly Roll (page 29). Then there is the roll as complex and grand as Bûche de Noël (page 64). Somewhere in between those two levels of expertise reside the rolls we have included in this grouping. There is a glorious Lemon Roll (page 31) that is filled with lemon cream, but might just as easily be filled with a judicious amount of orange buttercream. Ginger Walnut Roll (page 30) is filled with molasses-flavored whipped cream. Care is required to roll a sheet cake, but the process itself is very easy. For illustrations on how to guide the roll, see page 30, and then make rolled cakes part of your everyday baking repertoire.

BOSTON CREAM PIE

Yield:
one 9-inch cake

Equipment:
two 9-inch cake pans
upright electric mixer
8-inch cardboard
　round

Boston cream pie, not a pie at all, is often made with a batter to which hot milk is added. We've used sponge batter instead, with the layers separated by pastry cream and the whole topped with chocolate glaze. Boston cream pie is an American classic and rightfully so.

FOR THE CAKE

6 large eggs, separated, at room temperature	¼ teaspoon plus pinch of salt
1 cup granulated sugar	¼ teaspoon cream of tartar
1½ teaspoons vanilla	1 cup cake flour, sifted

1 recipe pastry cream (page 164) combined with 1 tablespoon rum or Cognac if desired

FOR THE CHOCOLATE GLAZE

2 tablespoons unsalted butter	2 tablespoons heavy cream
1 ounce semisweet chocolate, chopped coarse	½ cup confectioners' sugar
	1 teaspoon vanilla

Make the cake:

Butter the cake pans, line the bottoms with wax paper, and butter the paper. Dust the pans with flour, knocking out the excess.

In the bowl of the mixer beat the egg yolks until combined. Add ¾ cup of the granulated sugar, a little at a time, and beat the mixture until it falls in a thick ribbon when the beater is lifted (see illustration page 10). Beat in the vanilla and transfer the mixture to a bowl.

Preheat the oven to 350° F.

In the bowl of the mixer beat the egg whites with the pinch of salt until frothy. Add the cream of tartar and beat the whites until they hold soft peaks. Add the remaining ¼ cup granulated sugar, a little at a time, and beat the whites until stiff. Fold the whites into the batter gently but thoroughly. Sift the flour with the remaining ¼ teaspoon salt and fold it in batches into the egg mixture until just combined. Divide the batter between the cake pans and bake the layers in the middle of the oven for 20 to 25 minutes, or until a cake tester inserted in the centers comes out clean. Let the cakes cool in the pans on racks for 5 minutes. Invert them onto the racks, peel off the wax paper, and let cool.

Put 1 teaspoon of the pastry cream in the center of the cardboard round and arrange one of the cake layers on it. Spread the top of the layer with the pastry cream, smoothing it with a spatula, and set the second layer on top of it. Transfer the cake on the round to a cake plate.

Make the chocolate glaze:

In the top of a double boiler over simmering water melt the butter with the chocolate, stirring. Remove the pan from the heat and beat in the cream, confectioners' sugar, and vanilla and continue to beat until smooth.

Pour the glaze slowly and carefully over the top of the cake, smoothing it with a spatula and taking care not to let any of it drip down the sides of the cake. Serve the cake at room temperature.

GREAT AMERICAN JELLY ROLL

Yield:
one 15-inch rolled cake

Equipment:
jelly-roll pan, 15½ by 10½ by 1 inches
upright and hand-held electric mixers

This jelly roll, a clever variation on strawberry shortcake, makes a lovely light summer dessert and a perfect ending to a July Fourth celebration.

4 large eggs, separated, at room temperature
½ cup granulated sugar
1 teaspoon vanilla
1 tablespoon grated orange rind
½ teaspoon plus pinch salt
⅛ teaspoon cream of tartar
½ cup all-purpose flour, sifted

½ cup strawberry jam
⅔ cup well-chilled heavy cream
3 tablespoons confectioners' sugar plus additional for dusting
1 tablespoons orange-flavored liqueur if desired
1 cup strawberries, hulled and sliced

Butter the jelly-roll pan and line it with wax paper, leaving a 2-inch over-hang on each of the short sides. Butter the wax paper and dust it with flour, shaking out the excess. Preheat the oven to 400° F.

In the bowl of the upright mixer beat the egg yolks until combined. Add all but 2 tablespoons of the granulated sugar, a little at a time, and beat the mixture at medium speed for 3 to 4 minutes, or until light and creamy. Beat in the vanilla and 2 teaspoons of the orange rind and pour the batter into a large bowl.

In the bowl of the mixer beat the whites with the pinch of salt until frothy. Add the cream of tartar and beat the whites until they hold soft peaks. Add the reserved 2 tablespoons granulated sugar, a little at a time, and beat the whites until stiff. Fold the whites into the batter, gently but thoroughly. Sift the flour with the remaining salt and fold it in batches into the batter until the mixture is just combined.

Pour the batter into the pan, spread it evenly with a spatula, and bake the cake in the middle of the oven for 10 to 12 minutes, or until it pulls away from the sides of the pan and a cake tester inserted in the center comes out clean. Sift confectioners' sugar lightly over the top of the cake, cover the cake with wax paper and a baking sheet, and invert the cake on-to the baking sheet. Peel off the wax paper and trim any hardened edges from the sides of the cake. Cover the cake with a fresh piece of wax paper. Starting with a long side roll up the cake, lifting it with the wax paper and finishing with the seam side down (see illustrations on page 30). Let the cake cool completely.

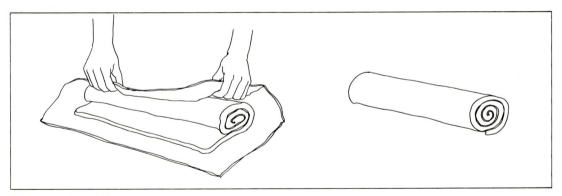

Rolling up a jelly roll

Unroll the cake, remove the paper, and spread the cake with the strawberry jam, leaving a ½-inch border at each of the short ends. In a chilled bowl with the hand-held mixer beat the cream with the remaining 3 tablespoons confectioners' sugar and the orange-flavored liqueur, if desired, until it holds soft peaks. With a spatula spread the cream on the cake, smoothing it into an even layer and leaving a 1-inch border on all sides. Scatter the strawberries over the cream, sprinkle them with the remaining orange rind, and roll up the cake. Transfer the jelly roll to a platter, seam side down, and trim the ends. Dust with sifted confectioners' sugar.

GINGER WALNUT ROLL WITH MOLASSES CREAM

Yield:
one 16-inch rolled
  cake

Equipment:
jelly-roll pan, 16 by 11
  by 1 inches
upright and hand-held
  electric mixers
pastry bag fitted with
  star tip

Make the cake:

FOR THE CAKE
7 large eggs, separated, at room
  temperature
⅓ cup granulated sugar

pinch of salt
¾ cup ground walnuts
2 teaspoons ground ginger

FOR THE MOLASSES CREAM
1½ teaspoons unflavored gelatin
3 tablespoons cold water
1½ cups well-chilled heavy cream

½ cup molasses
3 large walnut halves brushed with
  honey for garnish

Preheat the oven to 350° F. Butter the jelly-roll pan, line it with wax paper, and butter the paper.

In the bowl of the upright mixer beat the egg yolks until frothy. Gradually add the granulated sugar and continue to beat the mixture for 3 to 4 minutes, or until it falls in a ribbon when the beater is lifted (see illustration page 10).

In a bowl with the hand-held mixer beat the egg whites with the salt until they hold stiff peaks. Gently but thoroughly fold one fourth of the whites into the yolk mixture and pour the mixture over the remaining whites. Combine the ground walnuts and the ground ginger. Sprinkle the nut mixture over the egg mixture and gently fold the batter until there are no traces of white. Pour the batter into the jelly-roll pan, spreading it evenly with a metal spatula, and bake the cake in the middle of the oven for about 25 minutes, or until it is lightly browned and springy to the touch. Let the cake cool in the pan on a rack.

Make the molasses cream: In a small saucepan sprinkle the gelatin over the water and let it soften for 5 minutes. Heat the mixture over moderately low heat, stirring, until the gelatin is dissolved and the liquid is clear. In a chilled bowl with the mixer beat the heavy cream until it holds soft peaks, add the gelatin mixture in a stream and the molasses, beating, and beat the cream until it holds stiff peaks.

To assemble the roll: Loosen the wax paper from the side of the jelly-roll pan with a knife and invert the cake onto a baking sheet covered with a sheet of wax paper. Peel off the paper on top and spread the cake with the molasses cream, reserving ½ cup of it for garnish and leaving a 1-inch border. Starting with a long side, roll up the cake, lifting it with the wax paper and finishing with the seam side down (see illustrations page 30). Transfer the roll carefully to a platter. Fill the pastry bag with the reserved molasses cream and pipe it decoratively on top of the roll. Position the walnut halves on the cake.

LEMON ROLL

Yield:
one 15-inch rolled cake

Equipment:
jelly-roll pan, 15½ by 10½ by 1 inches
upright electric mixer

FOR THE LEMON CREAM
6 egg yolks
1 cup granulated sugar
½ cup fresh lemon juice, strained

1 tablespoon grated lemon rind
½ stick (¼ cup) unsalted butter, softened

FOR THE CAKE
4 large eggs, separated, at room temperature
1 tablespoon grated lemon rind
1 tablespoon fresh lemon juice, strained

1 cup granulated sugar
pinch of salt
pinch of cream of tartar
¼ cup cornstarch
¼ cup all-purpose flour

1 stick (½ cup) unsalted butter, softened

confectioners' sugar for dusting

Make the lemon cream: In a small heavy saucepan combine the egg yolks, granulated sugar, lemon juice, and rind and cook over moderate heat, stirring until thick. Do not let it boil. Remove the pan from the heat and stir in the butter, one tablespoon at a time. Transfer the mixture to a bowl and let it cool, covered with a buttered round of wax paper.

Make the cake:

Preheat the oven to 350° F. Butter the jelly-roll pan, line it with wax paper, leaving a 2-inch overhang on both of the short ends, and butter the paper.

In a large bowl beat the egg yolks with the lemon rind, the lemon juice, and ½ cup of the granulated sugar until the mixture falls in a ribbon when the beater is lifted (see illustration page 10). In the bowl of the mixer beat the egg whites with the salt until frothy, add the cream of tartar and beat the whites until they hold soft peaks. Beat in the remaining ½ cup granulated sugar, one tablespoon at a time, and beat the meringue until it holds stiff peaks.

Sift the cornstarch and flour together onto a sheet of wax paper. Fold one fourth of the meringue into the yolk mixture and fold in the remaining meringue alternately with the cornstarch mixture. Turn the batter into the jelly-roll pan, spreading it evenly, and bake the cake in the middle of the oven for 17 minutes, or until the paper pulls away easily from the ends of the cake. Leave the cake in the pan, cover it with a dampened dish towel, and let it cool on a rack.

In a bowl cream the butter. Beat in the lemon cream, a little at a time, and continue to beat the mixture until fluffy. Chill the filling, covered, for 30 minutes.

To assemble the lemon roll:

Dust a 16-inch length of wax paper with the confectioners' sugar. Remove the towel from the sheetcake and turn the cake out onto the wax paper. Peel the wax paper off the top of the cake and spread the cake with the lemon cream filling, leaving a 1-inch border on the long side farthest from you. Beginning with the long side nearest you, roll up the cake, lifting it with the wax paper (see illustrations page 30). Transfer the lemon roll, seam side down, to a serving board and dust it with the confectioners' sugar.

ANGEL FOOD AND CHIFFON CAKES

We all remember angel food cake for its extraordinary whiteness and chiffon cake for its exceptional lightness. How these qualities were arrived at wasn't important. The color of one and the texture of the other were what was memorable, and that both were brilliantly named.

We now know that the batter for angel food cake is based exclusively on egg whites that have been beaten to stiff, glossy peaks. Moreover, there is no fat or shortening in the mix. The cake is pristine and white because it started off that way. Angel food cake is a salient example of what can be achieved by the power of beaten whites, and all of the principals for whipping egg whites successfully apply.

We have also discovered that chiffon cake attains its lightness because oil—not butter or shortening—is used in the batter. Unlike angel food cake, egg yolks are also incorporated. It is the oil, though, that renders this cake light yet rich.

Each of the three cakes that follows bakes in a tube pan and has a specific method of cooling, with the pan suspended upside down on the neck of a bottle. The cake must be allowed to cool completely in this manner. To try to cool any of these cakes in the conventional manner, on a rack, will undo most of what was achieved during baking with the uniqueness of these respective batters.

ANGEL FOOD CAKE

Yield:
one 10-inch tube cake

Equipment:
upright electric mixer
10-inch tube pan

A good angel food cake is light and airy. You want to be sure to beat the egg whites—on which so much of the texture depends—to stiff peaks, and to combine the batter well, but not to overmix it. This grand cake, served with chocolate whipped cream, is one of those old-time favorites.

1¼ cups egg whites at room
   temperature
¼ teaspoon salt
1 teaspoon cream of tartar
1½ cups sugar

1 teaspoon vanilla
¼ teaspoon almond extract
1 cup sifted cake flour
1 recipe chocolate whipped cream
   (page 171) as an accompaniment

In the bowl of the mixer beat the egg whites with the salt until frothy. Add the cream of tartar and beat the whites until they hold soft peaks. Gently fold in the sugar, ¼ cup at a time, incorporating each addition before adding the next, and beat the whites until they hold stiff peaks. Fold in the vanilla and the almond extract.

Preheat the oven to 375° F.

Sift the flour 3 more times. Sift ¼ cup of the flour over the batter and fold it in quickly and lightly. Sift another ¼ cup flour over the batter and fold it in. Continue sifting and folding in the flour ¼ cup at a time until it is all folded into the batter, but do not overmix.

Pour the batter into the ungreased tube pan and bake the cake in the middle of the oven for 35 to 40 minutes, or until it springs back when pressed lightly with a finger. Remove the cake from the oven and suspend it upside down on the neck of a bottle. Let the cake cool completely.

With a sharp knife carefully loosen the cake from the sides and center tube of the pan. Tap the bottom of the pan firmly on the work surface to loosen the cake, and turn the cake out of the pan. Invert the cake onto a cake platter and serve it with the chocolate whipped cream.

COCONUT ANGEL FOOD CAKE WITH ORANGE FROSTING

Yield:
one 9-inch tube cake

Equipment:
upright electric mixer
9-inch tube pan

This angel food cake, which is slightly dressier than the preceding recipe, is covered with a superb orange frosting that is actually a variation on the much-beloved and ever-reliable seven-minute frosting.

FOR THE CAKE

8 egg whites at room temperature
½ teaspoon salt
½ teaspoon cream of tartar
1 cup superfine granulated sugar
½ teaspoon almond extract

½ teaspoon vanilla
¾ cup cake flour
1½ cups shredded unsweetened
  coconut

FOR THE ORANGE FROSTING

1¼ cups granulated sugar
2 egg whites
¼ cup fresh orange juice

1 tablespoon light corn syrup
1 teaspoon grated orange rind
pinch of salt

Make the cake:

In the bowl of the mixer beat the egg whites with the salt until frothy. Add the cream of tartar and beat the whites until they hold soft peaks. Sprinkle ½ cup of the superfine sugar over the whites, 2 tablespoons at a time, and continue to beat the whites until they hold stiff peaks. With a rubber spatula fold in the remaining ½ cup superfine sugar, 2 tablespoons at a time, the almond extract, and the vanilla.

Preheat the oven to 275° F.

Sift the cake flour 4 times onto a sheet of wax paper. Sift it over the egg whites, one fourth at a time, folding it lightly into the whites. Fold in ½ cup of the coconut. Pour the batter into the ungreased pan and bake the cake in the middle of the oven for 1½ hours. Remove the cake from the oven, suspend it upside down on the neck of a bottle, and let it hang for 1½ to 2 hours, or until cooled completely.

Increase the oven temperature to 350° F. Toast the remaining 1 cup coconut on a baking pan in the middle of the oven, shaking the pan occasionally, for 10 minutes. Let the coconut cool.

Make the orange frosting:

In the bowl of the mixer combine the granulated sugar, egg whites, orange juice, corn syrup, grated orange rind, and salt. Set the bowl over a saucepan containing 3 inches of boiling water and whisk the mixture until it is hot and foamy. Return the bowl to the mixer and beat the frosting at high speed for 7 minutes, or until it is cool and holds stiff peaks. Makes about 3 cups.

With a sharp knife release the cake from the sides and center tube of the pan and invert it onto a rack. Turn the cake right side up onto a cake plate and cover the sides and top with the orange frosting. Press the toasted coconut onto the sides of the cake.

CINNAMON WALNUT CHIFFON CAKE
WITH APPLE BUTTER FROSTING

Yield:
one 10-inch tube cake

Equipment:
upright electric mixer
10-inch tube pan
food processor fitted
  with steel blade

The chiffon cake is identifiable by the use of oil as opposed to butter in the batter. Because the oil is flavorless, you will note a lovely combination of spices and a fragrant apple butter frosting are used to give the cake its extraordinary flavor.

FOR THE CAKE

2¼ cups cake flour
1⅓ cups granulated sugar
1 tablespoon double-acting baking
  powder
1½ teaspoons cinnamon
1 teaspoon plus pinch of salt
¼ teaspoon freshly grated nutmeg
⅛ teaspoon ground cloves

6 egg yolks at room temperature
¾ cup apple juice
½ cup vegetable oil
1 teaspoon vanilla
½ teaspoon grated lemon rind
8 egg whites at room temperature
¼ teaspoon cream of tartar
⅔ cup finely chopped walnuts

FOR THE FROSTING

1½ sticks (¾ cup) unsalted butter,
  softened

1 cup confectioners' sugar, sifted
½ cup apple butter, or to taste

Make the cake:

Sift the flour, ¾ cup of the granulated sugar, the baking powder, cinnamon, 1 teaspoon of the salt, nutmeg, and cloves onto a sheet of wax paper. In a large bowl combine the egg yolks, apple juice, oil, vanilla, and lemon rind. Beat in the flour mixture until the batter is smooth.

Preheat the oven to 325° F.

In the bowl of the mixer beat the egg whites with the pinch of salt until frothy. Add the cream of tartar and beat the whites until they hold soft peaks. Add the remaining granulated sugar, a little at a time, and beat the whites until they hold stiff peaks. Stir one fourth of the whites into the yolk mixture and fold in the remaining whites and the walnuts.

Pour the batter into the ungreased tube pan and bake the cake in the middle of the oven for 1 hour, or until a cake tester comes out clean. Suspend the cake upside down on the neck of a bottle and let it cool completely. With a thin knife loosen the cake from the sides and center of the tube pan and invert the cake onto a rack.

Make the frosting:

In the food processor or in a blender put the butter, confectioners' sugar, and apple butter, turn on the motor, and blend the ingredients scraping down the sides of the container with a rubber spatula two or three times, until the frosting is smooth.

Spread the sides and top of the cake with the frosting and transfer the cake carefully to a cake stand.

LAYER CAKES

Who will ever forget having laid eyes for the very first time on a seven-layer cake? It just wasn't possible, all those thin, thin layers. It had to be magic, done by something other than man. As we have all grown up to learn, layer cakes are made by men and women—even seven-layer cakes—and indeed the same principals apply whether you are making two or seven layers.

For many of us, though, the magic of the layer cake never disappeared even with all that adult knowledge. It probably has something to do with the transformation of components. You start with two or three cake pans, a bowl of batter, and another of frosting. And when you are done you have a high-standing, captivating construct just waiting to be sliced.

Layer cakes can be plain or fancy, as both our Lady Baltimore (page 40) and Robert E. Lee (page 38) cakes demonstrate. Each obviously hails from the South, each is deservedly an American classic, and each is a grand, ele nt edifice. Other layer cakes are not nearly so highfalutin. With othe ver cakes it is the layers themselves that are simple—carrot cake, for , does not compare in complexity with a *génoise* layer, nor does the technical know-how to produce well.

W eptional about the layer cake, aside from the pure pleasure it l obvious number of guises it takes. You will find other wonde es of layer cakes in the *génoise* grouping in this chapter and in the te cake selections. We would also suggest you review the instructional text on cake-making at the beginning of this chapter to maximize the layer cake's full and singularly pleasing effect.

CARROT CAKE WITH CREAM CHEESE FROSTING AND MARZIPAN RABBITS AND CARROTS

Yield:
one 8-inch layer cake

While slightly less fanciful when undecorated, this remains a wonderful carrot cake, moist and spicy.

Equipment:
three 8-inch round cake pans
hand-held electric mixer

marzipan decorations (page 170) if desired

FOR THE CAKE
2 cups all-purpose flour
2 cups granulated sugar
2 teaspoons baking soda
1 teaspoon salt
1 tablespoon cinnamon

pinch of ground allspice
4 large eggs
1 cup vegetable oil
4 cups finely grated carrots (about 1 pound)

FOR THE FROSTING
1 pound cream cheese, softened
1 stick (½ cup) unsalted butter, softened

4 cups confectioners' sugar, sifted
2 teaspoons vanilla

½ cup apricot jam

Make the marzipan decorations the day you intend to serve the cake and let them dry overnight.

Make the cake:
Line the cake pans with wax paper and butter the paper. Dust the pans with flour and knock out the excess. Preheat the oven to 350° F.

Into a bowl sift together the flour, granulated sugar, baking soda, salt, cinnamon, and allspice. In a large bowl with the mixer beat the eggs for 1 minute, or until frothy, and add the oil in a stream, beating. Gradually beat in the flour mixture and beat the batter until it is just smooth. Stir in the carrots. Divide the batter among the cake pans, smoothing the tops, and bake the layers in the middle of the oven for 25 to 30 minutes, or until a cake tester inserted in the centers comes out clean. Let the layers cool in the pans on racks for 10 minutes. Run a thin knife around the edges of the cake pans and invert the layers onto the racks. Let the layers cool completely and peel off the wax paper.

Make the frosting:

The cake, undecorated, may be made up to 3 days ahead and chilled, covered. Let the cake come to room temperature before serving.

In a large bowl with the mixer cream together the cream cheese and the butter. Add the confectioners' sugar, a little at a time, beating, and beat in the vanilla.

Set one cake layer on a serving plate, spread half the apricot jam over it, and top it with another cake layer. Spread the layer with the remaining jam and top it with the remaining cake layer. Spread the frosting over the sides and top of the cake and garnish the cake with the marzipan decorations if desired.

ROBERT E. LEE CAKE

Coconut Cake with Lemon Filling

Yield:
one 8-inch layer cake

Equipment:
three 8-inch round
  cake pans
hand-held electric
  mixer
pastry brush
candy thermometer

We don't know if Robert E. Lee was devoted to coconut cake, but if he was this one would have had to have been his most preferred. Three layers and lemon filled, it is decorated with pristine coconut.

FOR THE CAKE

6 large eggs, separated, at room
  temperature
1 cup sugar
1 tablespoon grated orange rind
2 teaspoons grated lemon rind
2 teaspoons fresh orange juice

2 teaspoons fresh lemon juice
pinch of salt
¼ teaspoon cream of tartar
1 cup all-purpose flour sifted with ½
  teaspoon double-acting baking
  powder and ¼ teaspoon salt

FOR THE LEMON FILLING

4 egg yolks
⅓ cup sugar
½ stick (¼ cup) unsalted butter, cut
  into pieces

½ cup fresh lemon juice
2 teaspoons grated lemon rind

FOR THE FROSTING

¾ cup sugar
¼ cup water
4 egg whites at room temperature
pinch of salt
pinch of cream of tartar

1 tablespoon fresh lemon juice
1 tablespoon grated orange rind
2 teaspoons grated lemon rind
1 teaspoon vanilla

2 cups grated fresh coconut (for procedure page 174), or to taste

Make the cake:

Line the cake pans with wax paper and butter the paper. Dust the pans with flour and knock out the excess. Preheat the oven to 350° F.

In a large bowl with the mixer beat the egg yolks with ½ cup of the sugar until the mixture is lemon colored and falls in a ribbon when the beater is lifted (see illustration page 10). Stir in the orange rind, lemon rind, orange juice, and lemon juice. In a bowl with the mixer beat the egg whites with the pinch of salt until frothy, add the cream of tartar, and beat the whites until they hold soft peaks. Add the remaining ½ cup sugar, a little at a time, beating, and beat the meringue until it holds stiff peaks. Fold the meringue into the yolk mixture alternately with the flour mixture.

Divide the batter among the cake pans and bake the layers in the middle of the oven for 25 minutes, or until a cake tester inserted in the centers comes out clean. Let the layers cool in the pans on racks for 5 minutes, invert them onto the racks, and let them cool completely.

Make the lemon filling: In a heavy stainless steel or enameled saucepan combine the egg yolks, sugar, butter, and lemon juice. Cook the mixture over moderate heat, without letting it boil, whisking vigorously, until it thickens. Stir in the lemon rind, pour the mixture into a bowl, and let it cool. Chill the filling, covered with buttered wax paper, for at least 1 hour.

Make the frosting: In a small heavy saucepan combine the sugar with the water, bring the liquid to a boil, and boil it over moderate heat, stirring and washing down any sugar crystals clinging to the sides of the pan with the brush dipped in cold water, until it reaches the soft-ball stage, or the candy thermometer registers 234° F. In a bowl with the mixer beat the egg whites with the salt until frothy, add the cream of tartar, and beat the whites until they hold soft peaks. With the mixer running add the hot syrup in a stream and beat the meringue until it is completely cool. Beat in the lemon juice, orange rind, lemon rind, and the vanilla.

To assemble the cake: Set one of the layers on a cake plate and spread it with half the lemon filling. Top it with a second layer and spread it with the remaining filling. Top with the remaining cake layer. Spread the frosting on the sides and top of the cake, then press the grated fresh coconut lightly all over the entire frosting.

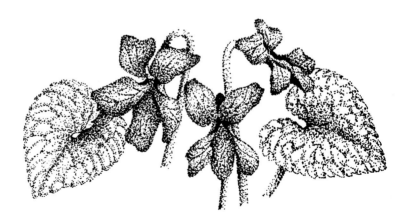

LADY BALTIMORE CAKE

Yield:
one 9-inch layer cake

Equipment:
three 9-inch round
  cake pans, 1 ½
  inches deep
upright electric mixer
pastry brush
candy thermometer

Some say this classic American cake originated in Maryland, others in Charleston, South Carolina. No matter. Its three light layers are filled with meringue that is studded with dried fruits and nuts. This is a superb Southern-style extravaganza, perfect for a special occasion.

2 cups chopped raisins

2 cups chopped walnuts

½ cup chopped dried figs

1 cup medium-dry Sherry

FOR THE CAKE

3 cups sifted cake flour

1 tablespoon double-acting baking
  powder

⅛ teaspoon salt

1½ sticks (¾ cup) unsalted butter,
  softened

1¾ cups sugar

1 cup milk

1 teaspoon almond extract

½ teaspoon vanilla

6 egg whites at room temperature

FOR THE ITALIAN MERINGUE

2 cups sugar

⅔ cup water

½ teaspoon cream of tartar

4 egg whites at room temperature

1 teaspoon vanilla

1 teaspoon almond extract

In a bowl combine the raisins, walnuts, and figs. Pour in the Sherry and let the mixture macerate, covered, at room temperature overnight.

Make the cake:

Flour the cake pans, knock out the excess flour, and line them with buttered rounds of wax paper. Preheat the oven to 375° F.

Into a bowl sift together the cake flour, baking powder, and salt. Sift the mixture 2 more times and set it aside.

In the bowl of the mixer cream the butter until light. Beat in the sugar, ¼ cup at a time, and continue to beat until light and fluffy. Stir in the dry ingredients alternately with the milk and beat the batter until smooth. Stir in the almond extract and the vanilla. In the bowl with the mixer beat the 6 egg whites until they hold stiff peaks and fold them gently but thoroughly into the batter.

Divide the batter among the cake pans and bake the layers in the middle of the oven for 25 minutes, or until the cakes pull away from the sides of the pans. Turn the layers out onto racks to cool and peel off the wax paper.

Make the Italian meringue:

In a saucepan combine the sugar, water, and cream of tartar. Cook the mixture over moderately low heat until the sugar is dissolved, washing down any sugar crystals clinging to the sides of the pan with the brush dipped in cold water. Raise the heat to moderately high and bring the syrup to a boil. Cook the syrup, undisturbed, until it reaches the soft-ball stage, or the candy thermometer registers 240° F. In the bowl of the mixer beat the egg whites until they hold stiff peaks and, beating constantly, pour the hot syrup into the whites in a stream. Continue to beat the meringue until it is lukewarm. Add the vanilla and the almond extract.

To assemble the cake: Drain the macerated fruits and nuts and fold them into the meringue. Set one of the cake layers on a cake plate. With a metal spatula spread the layer with ¾ cup of the meringue and top it with the second layer. Spread the second layer with the meringue in the same manner and top it with the third layer. Spread the remaining meringue over the sides and top of the cake, making decorative peaks.

CHOCOLATE CAKES

What distinguishes chocolate cake, aside from its popularity, which ranks it right up there with Coca-Cola as one of America's favorite sweets, is its many glorious interpretations. In fact, it is infrequent that two chocolate cakes are exactly the same. Chocolate itself has character, comes in different colors, and tastes unlike anything else in the world. It follows that chocolate cakes should have commensurate variety.

Baking succesfully with chocolate means melting it correctly. This can be done in several ways, but the most foolproof method melts it in the top of a double boiler over barely simmering, or hot, water. When melted, chocolate should be smooth and glossy. If heated to too high a temperature or over direct heat, chocolate seizes up and turns identifiably clumpy and granular. For all intents and purposes, chocolate is unusable if it has seized up. Don't embark upon such a reckless course. The well-being of a chocolate cake—not to mention the well-being of those who are going to enjoy it—is far too valuable to be tampered with like that.

CHOCOLATE ORANGE MARBLE CAKE

Yield:
1 cake

Equipment:
deep 1½-quart baking
  pan
hand-held and upright
  electric mixers

The combination of chocolate and orange is a classic one.

2 sticks (1 cup) unsalted butter,
  softened
1¼ cups sugar
2 large eggs, separated, plus 1 egg
  yolk, at room temperature
1¾ cups all-purpose flour
¾ teaspoon baking soda
¾ teaspoon double-acting baking
  powder

1 cup sour cream
the grated rind of 1 orange
2 ounces unsweetened chocolate,
  melted and cooled
pinch of cream of tartar
½ cup fresh orange juice

Butter the baking pan and line it with buttered wax paper. Preheat the oven to 350° F.

In the bowl of the upright mixer cream together the butter and 1 cup of the sugar until light. Add the egg yolks, one at a time, beating well after each addition. Into a bowl sift together the flour, baking soda, and baking powder. Add the flour mixture to the butter mixture alternately with the sour cream and beat until smooth.

Divide the cake batter between 2 bowls and into one stir the grated orange rind. Into the other bowl stir the melted chocolate. In a third bowl with the hand-held mixer beat the egg whites with the cream of tartar until they hold stiff peaks. Fold half the whites into the orange batter and half into the chocolate. Transfer the chocolate batter to the bowl with the orange batter and lightly swirl a spatula through the batters to marbleize the mixture. Pour into the baking pan and bake the cake in the middle of the oven for 1 hour and 10 minutes, or until a cake tester inserted in the center comes out clean. Transfer the cake to a rack and let it cool in the pan for 5 minutes.

In a bowl combine the orange juice with the remaining ¼ cup sugar and while the cake is still warm slowly pour the glaze over it. Let the cake cool completely, invert it onto a rack, and remove the wax paper. Invert the cake onto a board and serve it sliced.

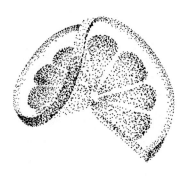

ARMAGNAC CHOCOLATE CAKE WITH PRUNES

Yield:
one 8½-inch cake

Equipment:
8½-inch round cake
  pan, 2 inches deep
hand-held electric
  mixer

You will note that there is no flour called for in this recipe. The leavening that does occur is triggered by the stiffly beaten egg whites. What you have, then, is a sensational combination of complex flavors and textures—chocolate, prunes, Armagnac, and pecans—in a single rich layer. This cake should be sliced thin and savored.

FOR THE CAKE

⅓ cup chopped pitted prunes
¼ cup Armagnac
6 ounces German sweet chocolate or
  semisweet chocolate, chopped
  coarse
3 tablespoons strong brewed coffee
1 stick (½ cup) unsalted butter, cut
  into bits and softened

3 large eggs, separated, at
  room temperature
½ cup plus 2 tablespoons granulated
  sugar
pinch of salt
pinch of cream of tartar
1 cup ground pecans
¼ cup cornstarch, sifted

FOR THE ICING

4 ounces German sweet chocolate or
  semisweet chocolate, chopped
  coarse
1 tablespoon Armagnac

3 tablespoons confectioners' sugar
½ stick (¼ cup) unsalted butter, cut
  into bits and softened

whole pecans for garnish

Make the cake:

In a small ceramic or glass bowl let the prunes macerate in the Armagnac for 30 minutes. Line the cake pan with wax paper and butter and flour the paper. Preheat the oven to 350° F.

In the top of a double boiler set over hot water melt the chocolate with the coffee. Remove the pan from the heat and beat in the butter, by bits, making sure that each piece is incorporated before adding the next.

In a large bowl with the mixer beat the egg yolks until smooth, add ½ cup of the granulated sugar, a little at a time, and beat the mixture until it falls in a ribbon when the beater is lifted (see illustration page 10). In a bowl with the mixer beat the egg whites with the salt until frothy, add the cream of tartar, and beat until they hold soft peaks. Gradually beat in the remaining 2 tablespoons granulated sugar and beat the whites until they hold stiff peaks.

Stir the chocolate mixture into the yolk mixture and add the pecans, the prunes and the Armagnac in which they macerated, and the cornstarch. Stir one third of the whites into the chocolate mixture and fold in the remaining whites until there are no traces of white. Spoon the batter into the pan and bake the cake in the middle of the oven for 40 minutes, or until a cake tester inserted 2 inches from the rim of the cake comes out clean (the center of the cake will remain moist). Transfer the cake in the pan to a rack and let it cool completely. Turn the cake out onto the rack, peel off the paper, and transfer the cake to a plate. Chill the cake for 1 hour, or until it is well chilled.

Make the icing:

In the top of the double boiler set over hot water heat the chocolate with the Armagnac until it is just melted. Remove the pan from the heat and stir in the confectioners' sugar. Stir in the butter, making sure that each piece is incorporated before adding the next.

Spread the sides and top of the cake with the chocolate icing and chill the cake until the icing is set. To serve, let the cake come to room temperature and decorate the top with the whole pecans.

CHOCOLATE MOUSSE CAKE WITH GANACHE ICING

Yield:
one 9-inch layer cake

Equipment:
two 9-inch round
  cake pans
upright mixer
pastry brush
candy thermometer
pastry bag fitted with
  medium fluted tip
8-inch cardboard
  round

This wonderful chocolate cake is layered with chocolate mousse and glazed with chocolate cream, or *crème ganache*. There is a subtle taste of orange to the whole and orange slices are employed as garnish. The cake is elegant and exciting and would befit any special occasion.

FOR THE CAKE

8 ounces semisweet chocolate, chopped
  coarse
¾ stick (6 tablespoons) unsalted
  butter, cut into tablespoons and
  softened
8 large eggs, separated, at room
  temperature

1 cup sugar
2 tablespoons orange-flavored liqueur
1 tablespoon grated orange rind
¼ teaspoon plus pinch of salt
pinch of cream of tartar
⅔ cup sifted cake flour

FOR THE CHOCOLATE MOUSSE

9 ounces semisweet chocolate, chopped
  coarse
6 egg yolks at room temperature
¾ cup plus 1 tablespoon sugar
2 tablespoons water

1¼ sticks (10 tablespoons) unsalted
  butter, cut into tablespoons and
  softened
2 tablespoons orange-flavored liqueur
4 egg whites at room temperature

FOR THE GANACHE ICING

1 cup heavy cream
8 ounces semisweet chocolate, chopped
  coarse

1 to 2 tablespoons orange-flavored
  liqueur

about 14 halved orange slices for garnish

Make the cake:

Butter the cake pans, line the bottoms with wax paper, and butter the paper. Dust the pans with flour and knock out the excess. Preheat the oven to 350° F.

In the top of a double boiler heat the chocolate over hot water, stirring, until just melted. Remove the pan from the heat and stir in the butter, one tablespoon at a time. Continue to stir the mixture until it is smooth and glossy.

In the bowl of the mixer beat the egg yolks until combined. Add ¾ cup of the sugar, a little at a time, and continue to beat the mixture until it falls in a ribbon when the beater is lifted (see illustration page 10). Beat in the melted chocolate mixture, the liqueur, and the orange rind. Transfer the mixture to a large bowl.

In the bowl of the mixer beat the egg whites with the pinch of salt until frothy. Add the cream of tartar and beat the whites until they hold soft peaks. Add the remaining ¼ cup sugar, a little at a time, and beat the whites until they are stiff. Sift the flour with the remaining ¼ teaspoon salt onto a sheet of wax paper. Stir one fourth of the whites into the batter. Fold in the remaining whites and sift and fold the flour mixture in batches into the egg mixture until just combined.

Pour the batter into the cake pans, smoothing the tops, and bake the layers in the middle of the oven for 30 to 35 minutes, or until a cake tester inserted into the centers comes out clean. Let the cakes cool in the pans on racks for 5 minutes, invert the cakes onto the racks, and remove the wax paper carefully. Let the cakes cool completely. (The cakes form a thin crust that will flake off.)

Make the chocolate mousse: In the top of the double boiler heat the chocolate over hot water, stirring until just melted.

In the bowl of the mixer beat the egg yolks until light and thick. In a small heavy saucepan combine the sugar with the water. Bring the mixture to a boil and boil it over moderate heat, stirring and washing down any sugar crystals clinging to the sides of the pan with the brush dipped in cold water until the syrup reaches the soft-ball stage, or the candy thermometer registers 238° F. With the mixer running add the hot syrup to the yolks in a stream, beating, and beat the mixture until it is completely cool. Beat in the butter, a little at a time, the melted chocolate, and the liqueur. Reserve one third of the mixture in a small bowl, covered. Chill the remaining mixture, covered, until firm.

In a large bowl with the mixer beat the egg whites with the salt until they hold soft peaks. Add the remaining 1 tablespoon sugar and beat the mixture until it just holds stiff peaks. Stir one fourth of the whites into the remaining chocolate mixture, fold in the remaining whites gently but thoroughly and chill the mousse, covered, until firm.

Make the *ganache* icing: In a small heavy saucepan bring the cream just to a simmer. Remove the pan from the heat, add the chocolate, and let the mixture stand, covered, for 5 minutes. Stir in the liqueur and continue to stir the *ganache* until smooth and tepid. Strain through a fine sieve into a small pitcher or a bowl with a lip.

To assemble the cake: Put 1 teaspoon of the mousse in the center of the 8-inch cardboard round and set one of the cake layers, bottom side up, on the cardboard.

Cover the cake with some of the mousse, smoothing it into an even layer, and top it with the remaining cake layer, bottom side up. Cover the top and sides of the cake with the remaining mousse, smoothing it with a spatula, and chill the cake until it is cold.

Set the cake on a rack over a jelly-roll pan and pour the *crème ganache* over it, smoothing it with a spatula to completely cover the top and sides of the cake. Let the cake stand at room temperature for 10 minutes and scrape any excess chocolate glaze from the jelly-roll pan back into the saucepan. Heat the excess *ganache*, stirring, until smooth, cool it to tepid, and pour it over the cake, smoothing it with a spatula over the top and sides of the cake. Chill the cake until the glaze is set.

Transfer the reserved chocolate mixture to the pastry bag. Arrange orange slices, rounded sides up, on the top of the cake, piping the buttercream along the base on each side of the slices. Arrange the remaining slices, rounded sides up, against the side of the cake and pipe the buttercream decoratively around the bottom edge of the cake.

Let the cake stand at room temperature for at least 15 minutes before serving.

Photo on page 100.

The cake may be prepared up to 2 days in advance and kept covered loosely with plastic wrap and chilled.

Pouring warm glaze

POUND AND BUNDT CAKES

We have grouped together pound and Bundt cakes for the simple reason that with the solitary exception of Sand Torte (page 48) all the batters incorporate considerable amounts of butter which, when properly creamed with sugar, will render an extraordinary crumb. Sand Torte, on the other hand, relies upon eggs and lots of air for its marvelous texture.

These kindred kinds of cake are curiously versatile. They easily grace a tea table and are equally at home in a picnic hamper.

CREAM CHEESE AND NUT POUND CAKE

Yield:
one 9-inch loaf cake

Equipment:
loaf pan, 9 by 5 by 3 inches
hand-held electric mixer

2 sticks (1 cup) unsalted butter, softened
1¼ cups sugar
3 ounces cream cheese, softened
4 large eggs at room temperature, beaten lightly
1½ teaspoons vanilla

2 cups cake flour, sifted
¼ teaspoon salt
1 teaspoon double-acting baking powder
1 cup finely chopped pecans, toasted and skins removed hazelnuts (for procedure page 174), or other nuts

Butter the loaf pan and dust it with flour, knocking out the excess. Preheat the oven to 350° F.

In a bowl with the mixer cream the butter. Gradually beat in the sugar and then the cream cheese, a little at a time, and continue to beat the mixture until fluffy. Add the eggs, one tablespoon at a time, and the vanilla and beat the mixture until well combined.

Sift the flour with the salt and baking powder and beat into the egg mixture, a little at a time, until smooth. Fold in the nuts. Pour the batter into the pan and smooth the top with a spatula. Bake the cake in the middle of the oven for 1 to 1¼ hours, or until a cake tester inserted in the center comes out clean. Let the cake cool in the pan on a rack for 5 minutes, turn it out onto the rack, and let it cool completely.

ORANGE POPPY SEED CAKE

Yield:
1 *Kugelhupf* cake

Equipment:
3-quart *Kugelhupf* mold
hand-held electric mixer

2 sticks (1 cup) unsalted butter, softened
1½ cups granulated sugar
4 large eggs
1¼ cups sour cream
⅓ cup poppy seeds
2 tablespoons grated orange rind

2 teaspoons vanilla
2½ cups all-purpose flour
1 teaspoon double-acting baking powder
¾ teaspoon baking soda
pinch of salt
sifted confectioners' sugar for dusting

Butter the *Kugelhupf* mold, dust it with flour, and shake out the excess flour. Preheat the oven to 350° F.

In a bowl with the mixer cream together the butter and granulated sugar until light and fluffy. Beat in the eggs, one at a time, beating well after each addition. Beat in the sour cream, the poppy seeds, the orange rind, and vanilla. Sift together the flour, baking powder, baking soda, and salt. Add to the egg mixture and combine the batter well. Pour into the mold and bake the cake in the middle of the oven for 1 hour and 10 to 15 minutes, or until a cake tester inserted halfway between the center and the rim comes out clean. Let the cake stand in the pan on a rack for 5 minutes, invert it onto the rack, and let it cool completely. Stand the cake upright and dust it with the sifted confectioners' sugar.

Photo on front cover and page 109.

SAND TORTE

Yield:
1 *Kugelhupf* cake

Equipment:
1½-quart *Kugelhupf* mold
upright electric mixer

Wonderful in texture due to the extraordinary amount of air beaten into the batter, this cake is the perfect accompaniment to fruit or ice cream.

¾ cup all-purpose flour
½ cup blanched almonds (for procedure page 174), toasted lightly and very finely ground
4 large eggs plus 2 egg yolks
½ cup granulated sugar

6 tablespoons clarified butter (page 164), cooled
1 teaspoon vanilla
½ teaspoon grated lemon rind
sifted confectioners' sugar for dusting

Butter the *Kugelhupf* mold, dust it with flour, and shake out the excess. Preheat the oven to 350° F.

Into a bowl sift together the flour and the ground almonds. In the bowl of the mixer combine the eggs, egg yolks, and the granulated sugar. Set the bowl over a saucepan containing 2 inches of hot but not boiling water and heat the mixture over low heat, stirring occasionally, until lukewarm (see illustration page 10). Transfer the bowl to the mixer and beat the mixture at high speed for 10 minutes, or until very light and triple in volume. Sift in the flour mixture, about ¼ cup at a time, folding in each portion lightly but thoroughly. Combine the clarified butter with the vanilla and the lemon rind and stir into the batter, about one tablespoon at a time. Pour the batter into the mold and bake the cake in the middle of the oven for 35 to 40 minutes, or until golden. Turn the cake out onto a rack and let it cool completely. Sift the confectioners' sugar over the top of the cake.

SCRIPTURE CAKE WITH MILK AND HONEY GLAZE

Yield:
1 Bundt cake

Equipment:
1½-quart ring mold
hand-held electric
    mixer
candy thermometer

All the ingredients in scripture cake, save the baking powder, of course, have references in the Bible. This spice cake, which is studded with dried fruits, has also been considered a fruitcake. Like fruitcake, it keeps well, carefully wrapped.

FOR THE CAKE

1 cup golden raisins
1 stick (½ cup) unsalted butter,
    softened
1 cup sugar
3 large eggs
3 tablespoons honey
1¾ cups all-purpose flour
2 teaspoons double-acting baking
    powder

½ teaspoon cinnamon
½ teaspoon ground allspice
¼ teaspoon freshly grated nutmeg
¼ teaspoon salt
a pinch of ground cloves
½ cup milk
1 cup chopped dried figs
½ cup sliced blanched almonds, lightly
    toasted

FOR THE GLAZE

1 cup sugar
¼ cup milk
1 tablespoon light corn syrup

1 tablespoon unsalted butter
¼ cup honey

Make the cake:

Put the raisins in a small bowl, cover them with hot water, and let them soak for 15 minutes.

Butter the ring mold, dust it with flour, and shake out the excess. Preheat the oven to 325° F.

In a large bowl with the mixer cream the butter. Add the sugar, a little at a time, beating, and beat until light and fluffy. Add the eggs, one at a time, beating well after each addition. Add the honey and combine the mixture well. Into a bowl sift together 1½ cups of the flour, the baking powder, cinnamon, allspice, nutmeg, salt, and cloves. Stir into the butter mixture alternately with the milk and combine the batter well.

Drain the raisins, pat them dry, and combine them with the figs, almonds, and the remaining ¼ cup flour. Toss the mixture well and fold it into the batter. Stir the batter well to incorporate the fruit mixture and spoon it into the ring mold. Smooth the top and rap the mold on a hard surface once or twice to expel any air bubbles. Bake the cake in the middle of the oven for 55 to 60 minutes, or until a cake tester inserted halfway between the edge and the center comes out clean. Transfer the cake to a rack and let it cool in the mold for 10 minutes. Invert the cake onto the rack and let it cool completely.

Make the glaze:

In a small heavy saucepan combine the sugar with the milk, corn syrup, and butter and bring the mixture to a boil over moderate heat, stirring until the sugar is dissolved. Boil the mixture, covered, for 1 minute. Uncover and boil it until the candy thermometer registers 238° F. Stir in the honey, bring the mixture to a boil, and boil it until the candy thermometer returns to 238° F. Remove from the heat and let the glaze cool, stirring constantly with a wooden spoon, until thickened slightly but still thin enough to drizzle over the cake (the glaze will turn opaque as it cools). If necessary, reheat the glaze over low heat, stirring, to thin it to the desired consistency. Makes about 1 cup.

Wrap the cake tightly in plastic wrap and store it in an airtight container for up to 4 days.

Put the cake on the rack over wax paper and drizzle the glaze evenly over it, letting it run down the sides. Let the cake stand until the glaze has set and transfer it with metal spatulas to a cake plate.

COFFEECAKES

For organizational purposes, we have grouped coffeecakes and a yeast cake together. That they are entirely different in composition is obvious. That there are coffeecakes much better suited for tea than for breakfast is less obvious, and that there are yeast cakes much better suited for dessert even less so. What constitutes a good morning cake? What, on the other hand, constitutes a good tea cake? Something simple and subtle in flavor we would suspect. And while yeast cakes, and particularly bread, are expected at breakfast, not all yeast cakes are appropriate at that early morning hour.

Our collection of coffeecakes, all leavened with baking powder or baking soda or both is short; the cakes are simple, and the flavors are subtle and pleasing. An easy-to-make cake such as Cinnamon Cake (page 51) would readily enhance a tea cart. So would Blueberry Pecan Crumb Cake (page 52), with its brown sugar-nut topping. Pumpkin Sour Cream Coffeecake (page 53) would not only accompany a cup of tea well, but it might also be a wonderful offering at a fall tailgate picnic. So even though these are called coffeecakes and we associate coffee and cake in the morning, they should not be relegated to breakfast any more than "quick" bread should be thought of as bread.

At the mention of yeast, some people quake in their boots. It is complicated and alive and has to be proofed, they mumble. And anyway, how can you tell when it's ready? they ask. Yeast takes too long, someone else chimes in. There is some truth to all of this. Yeast is alive and, for precautionary reasons—for the simple purpose of finding out if it is going to work—should be proofed. To proof is to dissolve the yeast in warm water, checking for bubbles and foam as "proof" that the yeast is active and alive. And yes, a cake made with yeast does take longer to make, because the dough must be left to rise. That happens to be part of the great appeal of working with a yeast dough, however.

Were we asked the question, What is in a name as regards the recipes that follow? we would reply adaptability.

CINNAMON CAKE

Yield:
one 9-inch square cake

Equipment:
9-inch square cake pan, 2 inches deep
hand-held electric mixer

1¼ cups sugar
½ teaspoon cinnamon
2 sticks (1 cup) unsalted butter, cut into pieces and softened
2 large eggs, beaten lightly
2½ cups all-purpose flour

4 teaspoons double-acting baking powder
½ teaspoon salt
1¼ cups milk
⅓ cup cinnamon sugar (page 166)

Butter and flour the cake pan, knocking out the excess flour. Preheat the oven to 350° F.

In a bowl combine the 1¼ cups sugar with the cinnamon. Add the butter and cream the mixture with the mixer until very light. Beat in the eggs. In another bowl sift together the flour, baking powder, and salt. Add ½ cup of the dry ingredients at a time to the egg mixture alternately with the milk and combine until smooth. Pour the batter into the cake pan, spread it evenly with a metal spatula, and bake the cake in the middle of the oven for 45 minutes, or until well browned and a cake tester inserted in the center comes out clean. Let the cake cool on a rack for 5 minutes.

Sprinkle the cinnamon sugar over the still-warm cake. Cut the cake into squares and serve it warm.

BLUEBERRY PECAN CRUMB CAKE

Yield:
1 cake, 13 by 9 inches

Equipment:
baking pan, 13 by 9 inches
hand-held electric mixer

FOR THE CAKE

½ stick (¼ cup) unsalted butter, softened
¼ cup vegetable shortening at room temperature
1 cup sugar
3 large eggs, beaten lightly
1¾ cups plus 1 tablespoon all-purpose flour

1 teaspoon double-acting baking powder
1 teaspoon baking soda
¼ teaspoon salt
1 cup sour cream
1 tablespoon grated lemon rind
3 cups blueberries, picked-over

FOR THE TOPPING

1 cup firmly packed light brown sugar
¼ cup all-purpose flour
½ cup finely chopped pecans

½ stick (¼ cup) unsalted butter, cut into bits

Make the cake:

Butter the baking pan, dust it with flour, and knock out the excess flour. Preheat the oven to 350° F.

In a large bowl with the mixer cream the butter and the shortening. Add the sugar, a little at a time, beating, and beat until light and fluffy. Beat in the eggs, one at a time, beating well after each addition. Into another bowl sift together the 1¾ cups flour, the baking powder, baking soda, and salt. Add the dry ingredients to the egg mixture alternately with the sour cream, stirring until the batter is just combined. Fold in the lemon rind. Toss the blueberries with the remaining 1 tablespoon flour and add to the batter. Spread the batter in the baking pan.

Make the topping:

In a small bowl combine the brown sugar with the flour and pecans and blend in the butter until the mixture resembles coarse meal.

Sprinkle the topping evenly over the batter and bake the cake in the middle of the oven for 50 minutes, or until a cake tester inserted in the center comes out clean. Let the cake cool in the pan on a rack for 10 minutes, cut it into squares, and transfer it to a platter.

PUMPKIN SOUR CREAM COFFEECAKE

Yield:
one 8-inch cake

Equipment:
8-inch square baking
  pan
hand-held electric
  mixer

A splendid offering for the fall, this cake combines pumpkin, sour cream, and spices, plus a nutted brown sugar topping.

FOR THE CAKE

1/3 cup granulated sugar
1/2 stick (1/4 cup) unsalted butter, softened
1/3 cup fresh or canned pumpkin purée
1/4 cup sour cream
1 large egg, beaten lightly
1 1/2 tablespoons grated orange rind

1 1/4 cups sifted all-purpose flour
1 tablespoon double-acting baking powder
1/2 teaspoon baking soda
1/4 teaspoon freshly grated nutmeg
1/2 teaspoon salt
1/3 cup milk

FOR THE STREUSEL TOPPING

1/4 cup firmly packed light brown sugar
3 tablespoons cold unsalted butter, cut into bits

2 tablespoons granulated sugar
2 tablespoons all-purpose flour
1/2 teaspoon cinnamon
1/3 cup chopped walnuts

Make the cake:

Butter the baking pan. Preheat the oven to 375° F.

In a large bowl with the mixer cream together the sugar and the butter. Add the pumpkin purée, sour cream, egg, and orange rind and beat until well combined. Into another bowl sift together the flour, baking powder, baking soda, nutmeg, and salt. Stir the flour mixture into the pumpkin mixture alternately with the milk and blend until just combined. Pour the batter into the pan.

Make the streusel topping:

In a small bowl combine the brown sugar, butter, granulated sugar, flour, and cinnamon and blend the mixture until it resembles coarse meal. Sprinkle the streusel evenly over the batter and top it with the walnuts.

Bake the coffeecake in the middle of the oven for 45 minutes, or until a cake tester inserted in the center comes out clean. Let the cake cool in the pan on a rack for 10 minutes and cut it into squares. Serve the cake warm or at room temperature.

STREUSEL PLUM CAKE

Yield:
one 10-inch cake

Equipment:
upright electric mixer
  fitted with the
  dough hook
  (optional)
one 10-inch round
  cake pan or piece of
  cardboard
pastry brush

Make the cake:

Make the topping:

Purple plums with a sugar topping on a sweetened yeast dough base—an unusually good combination of textures and flavors.

FOR THE CAKE
1½ teaspoons active dry yeast
2 tablespoons lukewarm water
¼ cup plus pinch of granulated sugar
2 cups all-purpose flour

½ teaspoon salt
½ cup milk
½ stick (¼ cup) unsalted butter
1 egg yolk

FOR THE TOPPING
1 pound small purple plums, pitted
  and quartered
⅓ cup all-purpose flour
¼ cup granulated sugar

3 tablespoons unsalted butter, softened
⅛ teaspoon cinnamon
1 egg white, beaten lightly, for egg
  wash

sifted confectioners' sugar for dusting

In a small bowl proof the yeast in the water with the pinch of sugar for 15 minutes, or until foamy.

Into a large bowl sift together the flour, the remaining ¼ cup sugar, and the salt. In a saucepan combine the milk with the butter, heat the mixture over moderate heat until the butter is melted, and let it cool to lukewarm. Lightly beat the egg yolk with a little of the milk mixture and add it and the yeast to the flour mixture. Gradually add the remaining milk mixture and blend to form a dough. With the dough hook of the electric mixer, or with a wooden spoon, beat the dough until smooth and elastic and no longer sticky. Put the dough into a lightly buttered bowl, turn to coat it with the butter, and let it rise in a warm place, loosely covered, for 1½ hours, or until double in bulk.

Butter a baking sheet well and on it, using the cake pan, trace a 10-inch circle. Punch down the dough, roll it on a floured surface into a 10-inch circle, and arrange it on the baking sheet, stretching it to fit the outline and making a 1-inch rim. Let the dough rise, loosely covered, for 30 minutes.

Preheat the oven to 400° F.

Arrange the plums, skin side down, in concentric circles on the dough.

In a bowl blend the flour, granulated sugar, butter, and cinnamon with a fork until the mixture forms crumbs. Sprinkle the streusel over the plums. Brush the edge of the dough with the lightly beaten egg white and bake the cake in the middle of the oven for 10 minutes. Reduce the oven temperature to 375° F. and bake the cake for 30 minutes more, or until the edge is golden. Let the cake cool on the baking sheet for 10 minutes, remove it carefully to a rack, and let it cool completely. Just before serving, sprinkle the cake with the confectioners' sugar.

CAKES WITH FRUITS

There are cakes that we have known about and liked ever since child-hood—certain birthday cakes, for example, and other favorite layer cakes, like carrot, perhaps. Included among this nostalgic category are several of our cakes made with fruit: Strawberry Shortcakes (page 59), and two up-side-down cakes. What these classic cakes have in common that renders them so satisfying is in large part their simplicity. One is made with bis-cuits and berries in fresh fruit syrup. Another is the very sweet concept of fruit on the bottom and cake on the top that someone was then clever enough to reverse. The ideas are very simple and straightforward and honest. These cakes, like the others in this grouping, are easy to like.

GLAZED APPLE CAKE

Yield:
one 9-inch cake

Equipment:
food mill fitted with
    fine disk
9-inch springform pan

3 large McIntosh apples (about 1½ pounds), cored and quartered
¼ cup water
2-inch strip of lemon peel
1 stick (½ cup) unsalted butter, softened
1 cup sugar
1 large egg
2¼ cups all-purpose flour

2 teaspoons baking soda
1 teaspoon cinnamon
½ teaspoon freshly grated nutmeg
¼ teaspoon ground cloves
¼ teaspoon salt
½ cup finely chopped pecans, toasted
2 Granny Smith apples
¼ cup apricot jam, strained
whipped cream as an accompaniment

In a stainless steel or enameled saucepan combine the McIntosh apples with the water and lemon peel, bring the water to a boil, and simmer the apples, covered, for 20 minutes, or until tender. Cook the mixture, un-covered, over moderately high heat, stirring, until the water is almost evaporated. Force the mixture through the food mill into a bowl and let the purée cool.

Generously butter the springform pan and preheat the oven to 350° F.

In a large bowl cream the butter, beat in the sugar, and beat the mixture until light and fluffy. Beat in the egg and the apple purée. Into a bowl sift together the flour, baking soda, cinnamon, nutmeg, cloves, and salt. Stir the flour mixture and the pecans gently into the apple mixture and pour the batter into the springform pan.

Peel and core the Granny Smiths, halve them lengthwise, and cut them crosswise into thin slices. Arrange the apple slices decoratively in bunches on the batter, pressing them slightly into the batter. Bake the cake in the middle of the oven for 1¼ hours, or until a cake tester inserted in the center comes out clean. Remove the cake to a rack.

In a small saucepan melt the jam over low heat, brush it over the cake, and let the cake cool in the pan on a rack for 20 minutes. Run a sharp knife around the edge of the pan to loosen the cake and remove the sides of the pan. Serve the cake warm or at room temperature with the whipped cream.

Photo on page 101.

Variation:

GLAZED PEAR CAKE: Substitute 3 large firm but ripe pears to make the fruit purée. Use 2 firm but ripe unpeeled pears, halved lengthwise, cored, and cut into thin slices for the top of the cake.

CHERRY KUCHEN

Yield:
one 8-inch square cake

Equipment:
8-inch square baking pan
pastry blender (optional)

2 cups all-purpose flour
¾ cup plus 2 tablespoons sugar
¼ teaspoon double-acting baking powder
¼ teaspoon salt
1 stick (½ cup) unsalted butter

1 teaspoon cinnamon
1½ pounds sweet cherries, stemmed and pitted
2 egg yolks
1 cup sour cream

Preheat the oven to 400° F.

Into a bowl sift together the flour, the 2 tablespoons sugar, baking powder, and salt. Cut in the butter with the pastry blender or with two knives until the mixture is mealy. Press the dough on the bottom and half-way up the sides of the baking pan.

In a bowl combine the cinnamon and the remaining ¾ cup sugar. Arrange the cherries on the dough, sprinkle the cinnamon-sugar over them, and bake the kuchen in the middle of the oven for 15 minutes. In a bowl combine the egg yolks with the sour cream, pour the mixture over the cherries, and bake the kuchen for 30 minutes more. Transfer the cake in the pan to a rack and let it cool for 10 minutes. Cut the cake into squares and serve it while still warm.

PLUM AND NECTARINE UPSIDE-DOWN CAKE

Yield:
one 9-inch cake

Equipment:
hand-held electric
  mixer
non-stick 9-inch
  round cake pan or
  non-stick 10-inch
  ovenproof skillet

1 stick (½ cup) unsalted butter,
  softened
¾ cup sugar
1 large egg, beaten lightly
1 cup all-purpose flour
1 teaspoon double-acting baking
  powder
¼ teaspoon salt

⅓ cup milk
2 tablespoons brandy
1 teaspoon vanilla
2 plums, pitted and sliced thin
1 nectarine, pitted and sliced thin
lightly whipped cream as an
  accompaniment if desired

Preheat the oven to 350° F.

In a bowl with the mixer cream 6 tablespoons of the butter, add ½ cup of the sugar, and beat the mixture until light and fluffy. Beat in the egg. In another bowl sift together the flour, baking powder, and salt. Add the flour mixture to the butter mixture alternately with the milk, beating until the batter is smooth, and beat in the brandy and vanilla.

In the cake pan or skillet melt the remaining 2 tablespoons butter over moderately low heat, stir in the remaining ¼ cup sugar, and cook the mixture, stirring gently, for 2 minutes. Remove the pan from the heat and in the bottom of the pan arrange the plum and nectarine slices decoratively, overlapping them slightly. Return the pan to the heat and cook the mixture, undisturbed, for 2 to 3 minutes, or until the fruit begins to give up its juices. Remove the pan from the heat, spoon the batter carefully and evenly over the fruit, and bake the cake in the middle of the oven for 30 to 40 minutes, or until a cake tester inserted in the center comes out clean.

Let the cake cool in the pan on a rack for 10 minutes, invert a serving plate over the pan, and invert the cake onto it. Serve the cake warm or at room temperature with the whipped cream if desired.

CRANBERRY UPSIDE-DOWN CAKE

Yield:
one 9-inch cake

Equipment:
9-inch round cake
 pan, 1½ inches deep
hand-held electric
 mixer
pastry brush

Here is a wonderful finale to the Thanksgiving Day dinner.

*¾ stick (6 tablespoons) plus 3
  tablespoons unsalted butter,
  softened*
1 cup sugar
*1 pound cranberries, rinsed, picked
  over, and patted dry*
1 large egg
1 teaspoon vanilla
1 teaspoon minced orange rind

1¼ cups all-purpose flour
*1½ teaspoons double-acting baking
  powder*
¼ teaspoon salt
½ cup milk
⅓ cup red currant jelly
*sweetened whipped cream as an
  accompaniment if desired*

Preheat the oven to 350° F.

Butter the bottom and sides of the cake pan with the 3 tablespoons butter, sprinkle ½ cup of the sugar evenly over the bottom, and arrange the cranberries in the pan.

In a bowl with the mixer cream together the remaining ¾ stick butter and ½ cup sugar. Add the egg, vanilla, and orange rind and beat the mixture until well combined.

Into another bowl sift together the flour, baking powder, and salt. Stir the dry ingredients into the butter mixture, ½ cup at a time, alternately with the milk and stir the batter until it is just combined. Pour the batter over the cranberries and smooth the top. Bake the cake on a baking sheet in the middle of the oven for 1 hour, or until well browned. Transfer the cake to a rack and let it cool in the pan for 20 minutes. Run a thin knife around the inside of the pan and invert the cake onto a cake stand.

In a small saucepan melt the currant jelly over low heat, stirring, and brush it over the cake. Serve the cake warm or at room temperature with the whipped cream if desired.

STRAWBERRY SHORTCAKES

Yield:
8 servings

Equipment:
3-inch round cutter
pastry brush

Cream biscuits with just a touch of lemon are split, lightly buttered, then filled with a splendid strawberry syrup. These shortcakes are marvelous and very easy to make.

3 pints strawberries, hulled, plus 8 small unhulled berries for garnish
½ cup plus 2 tablespoons sugar
¼ cup fresh lemon juice plus additional to taste
2 cups all-purpose flour
1 tablespoon double-acting baking powder

½ teaspoon salt
2 tablespoons unsalted butter, cut into bits, plus butter for spreading
1½ teaspoons minced lemon rind
¾ to 1 cup heavy cream
milk for brushing the biscuits
lightly whipped cream as an accompaniment

Chop 1 pint of the strawberries. In a stainless steel or enameled saucepan combine them with the ½ cup sugar and the ¼ cup lemon juice. Bring the liquid to a boil and cook the mixture over moderately high heat, stirring, for 10 minutes, or until it is thickened and reduced to about 1¼ cups. Pour the mixture into a bowl and let it cool completely. Slice the remaining 2 pints strawberries, stir them into the cooked strawberries, and add lemon juice to taste. Let the mixture stand for 1 hour.

Butter a baking sheet and preheat the oven to 400° F.

Into a bowl sift together the flour, the remaining 2 tablespoons sugar, baking powder, and salt. Blend in the 2 tablespoons butter and the lemon rind with your fingertips until the mixture resembles coarse meal. Stir in enough of the heavy cream to make a soft dough. Form the dough into a ball and roll or pat it out ½ inch thick on a floured surface. Cut out rounds with the cutter dipped in flour and arrange them on the baking sheet 2 inches apart. Form the dough scraps gently into a ball, repeat the procedure, and arrange the rounds on the baking sheet. Brush the tops of the rounds lightly with the milk. Bake the biscuits in the middle of the oven for 15 to 20 minutes, or until puffed and golden.

Split the biscuits horizontally with a fork and while they are still warm spread the halves with the remaining butter. Mound the bottom halves of the biscuits with the strawberry mixture and top the berries with the biscuit tops. Arrange the shortcakes on a platter, garnish them with whole berries, and serve them with the whipped cream.

Variation:

BLUEBERRY SHORTCAKES: In a saucepan combine 1 pint blueberries, picked over, with ½ cup sugar and 1 tablespoon fresh lemon juice. Cook the berries, covered, over low heat for 5 minutes. Remove the cover and reduce the juices over high heat until thickened. Transfer the syrup to a bowl, let cool, and stir in 2 cups fresh blueberries.

Make biscuits as described above and form shortcakes with the blueberry syrup. Serve with whipped cream.

CAKES FOR SPECIAL OCCASIONS

The cakes that have preceded these for special occasions are hardly every-day cakes. There is nothing whatsoever usual or commonplace about Cassata (page 20), or Kaisertorte (page 24), or Chocolate Mousse Cake with Ganache Icing (page 44). Each is an extraordinary combination, and the only thing everyday about any of them might be that we would proba-bly like to have a little of each of them every day.

With that said, this selection of cakes for special occasions that fol-lows is admittedly arbitrary, and there is no reason why, with the obvious exceptions of the highly traditional and seasonal Bûche de Noël, you could not serve any of these cakes anytime you desired.

This small collection includes two fruitcake recipes—a white fruit-cake and a dark, rich, many-fruited combination. If you are thinking of preparing the dark fruitcake as a Christmas gift, be sure to build into your own calendar the number of weeks it will need to mellow.

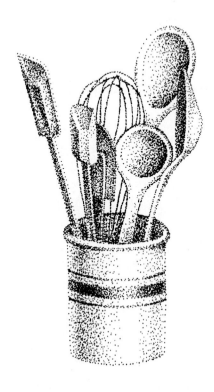

REFRIGERATOR CHEESECAKE

Yield:
one 10-inch cake

Equipment:
10-inch springform pan
hand-held electric mixer

This cheesecake is not baked. Instead it relies on gelatin and a good chill to achieve its luscious texture.

1 graham cracker crust (page 74), made with 2 additional tablespoons unsalted butter and ½ teaspoon cinnamon added
4 large eggs, separated, at room temperature
1 cup sugar
1 cup heavy cream, scalded
1½ pounds cream cheese, softened

1½ teaspoons grated lemon rind
1½ teaspoons vanilla
1 tablespoon unflavored gelatin
¼ cup fresh lemon juice
pinch of salt
⅛ teaspoon cream of tartar
1 cup sour cream
fresh fruit for garnish if desired

Preheat the oven to 350° F. Generously butter the springform pan.

Press the graham cracker crumb crust mixture onto the bottom and sides of the springform pan and bake in the lower third of the oven for 10 minutes. Let the crust cool.

In a bowl with the mixer beat the egg yolks until smooth, add ¾ cup of the sugar, and beat the mixture until it falls in a ribbon when the beater is lifted (see illustration page 10). Add the hot cream in a stream and beat until combined. Transfer the yolk mixture to a heavy saucepan and cook it over moderately low heat without lettting it boil, stirring until it is thick enough to coat a spoon. Pour the yolk mixture into a bowl and let it cool.

In a large bowl with the mixer beat the cream cheese until smooth. Add the yolk mixture, lemon rind, and vanilla and beat until combined.

In a small bowl let the gelatin soften in the lemon juice for 5 minutes. Set the bowl in a larger bowl of hot water and stir the gelatin until dissolved. Add the gelatin mixture to the cream cheese mixture and chill the filling, covered loosely, until cold, but do not let it set.

In a bowl with the mixer beat the egg whites with the salt until frothy, add the cream of tartar, and beat the whites until they hold soft peaks. Add the remaining ¼ cup sugar, a little at a time, and beat the whites until stiff. Stir one fourth of the whites into the cream cheese mixture and fold in the remaining whites. Fold in the sour cream. Pour the filling into the crust. Chill the cheesecake, covered loosely, for at least 3 hours or overnight.

Garnish the cheesecake with fresh fruit if desired.

WHITE FRUITCAKE WITH ICING

Yield:
1 loaf cake, 12 by 4½ by 3 inches

Equipment:
loaf pan, 12 by 4½ by 3 inches
hand-held and upright electric mixers
candy thermometer

We all recognize dark fruitcakes, rich with dried fruits and doused in spirits. White fruitcakes by comparison are infinitely lighter, much more cake-like, and by all rights should be served at other times of the year besides the Christmas holidays. Try this appealing one in the spring.

FOR THE CAKE

½ cup sugar
½ stick (¼ cup) unsalted butter, softened
3 large eggs
3 cups all-purpose flour
1 tablespoon double-acting baking powder

½ teaspoon baking soda
½ teaspoon salt
1 cup buttermilk
2 cups diced glacéed mixed fruits

FOR THE ICING

2½ cups sugar
1½ cups water
3 tablespoons grated orange rind
3 egg whites at room temperature

pinch of cream of tartar
1½ teaspoons vanilla
1 to 2 teaspoons boiling water, if needed

Make the cake:

Butter the loaf pan, dust it with flour, and knock out the excess flour. Preheat the oven to 325° F.

In a large bowl with the mixer cream together the sugar and the butter until light and fluffy. Add the eggs, one at a time, beating well after each addition. Into a bowl sift together the flour, baking powder, baking soda, and salt. Stir the dry ingredients into the butter mixture alternately with the buttermilk. Fold in the glacéed fruits, combining the batter well. Pour the batter into the loaf pan and bake the cake in the middle of the oven for 1 to 1¼ hours, or until a cake tester inserted in the center comes out clean.

Let the cake cool in the pan on a rack for 15 minutes, invert it onto the rack, and let it cool completely.

Make the icing:

In a saucepan combine the sugar, water, and grated orange rind. Bring the mixture to a boil over moderate heat, stirring until the sugar is dissolved, and cook the syrup until the candy thermometer registers 240° F.

In the large bowl of the upright mixer beat the egg whites with the cream of tartar until they hold soft peaks. Pour in the syrup in a stream, beating, and beat the mixture until the icing is fluffy and well combined. Stir in the vanilla.

Spread the sides and top of the cake with the icing, beating in the boiling water if the icing becomes too firm to spread, and let the cake stand until the icing is set.

SPICED BLACK FRUITCAKE

Yield:
2 fruitcakes, 9 by 5 by 3 inches

Equipment:
2 loaf pans, 9 by 5 by 3 inches
cheesecloth
tightly covered containers for storage

This dense dark fruitcake requires at least a month to age. Plan ahead if you intend to give it as a Christmas present.

1 pound dried currants
12 ounces raisins
12 ounces golden raisins, chopped
12 ounces dried figs, chopped
8 ounces dried pitted prunes, stewed, drained, and chopped
8 ounces pitted dates, chopped
8 ounces slivered blanched almonds, toasted
6 ounces glacéed cherries, finely sliced
6 ounces citron, finely sliced
4 ounces candied orange peel (page 168), finely shredded

3 cups dark rum plus rum for soaking the cheesecloth
2 sticks (1 cup) unsalted butter, softened
2 cups firmly packed dark brown sugar
1½ teaspoons cinnamon
1½ teaspoons freshly grated nutmeg
1½ teaspoons ground allspice
5 large eggs
2 cups sifted all-purpose flour
2 teaspoons double-acting baking powder
½ teaspoon salt

In a large bowl combine the currants, raisins, golden raisins, figs, prunes, dates, almonds, glacéed cherries, citron, and candied orange peel. Stir in the 3 cups dark rum and let the mixture macerate, covered, stirring it every other day, for 1 week.

Preheat the oven to 275° F. Butter the baking pans, line them with brown paper or wax paper, and butter the paper lightly.

In a bowl with the mixer cream the butter and gradually blend in the brown sugar, cinnamon, nutmeg, and allspice. Beat in 2 of the eggs. Into a large bowl sift the flour, baking powder, and salt. Blend 1 cup of the flour mixture into the creamed mixture and beat in the remaining 3 eggs. Stir in the fruits and the rum in which they macerated. Add the remaining flour mixture and combine the batter well.

Pour the batter into the pans, pressing it firmly into the corners. Put a shallow pan filled with hot water on the bottom of the oven under the cake pans and bake the cakes in the middle of the oven for 2½ hours, or until a cake tester inserted in the center comes out clean. Cool the cakes in the pans on racks for 1 hour.

While the cakes are cooling, soak cheesecloth in dark rum.

Transfer the cakes to racks, peel off the paper, and let the cakes cool completely. Wrap the cakes in the cheesecloth and store them in the containers. Moisten the cloths occasionally with the remaining dark rum and let the cakes age for at least 1 month.

BÛCHE DE NOËL

Yule Log

Yield:
one 15-inch rolled
cake

Equipment:
jelly-roll pan, 15½ by
10½ by 1 inches
upright and hand-held
electric mixers
pastry brush
candy thermometer

FOR THE CAKE

4 large eggs, separated, plus 2 egg
whites, at room temperature
½ cup granulated sugar
1 tablespoon eau-de-vie de
framboise (raspberry brandy)
¼ teaspoon salt

¼ teaspoon cream of tartar
½ cup sifted all-purpose flour
¼ cup sifted unsweetened cocoa
powder plus additional sifted cocoa
powder for dusting the cake

FOR THE CHOCOLATE BUTTERCREAM

6 egg yolks
⅔ cup granulated sugar
¼ cup water
3 sticks (1½ cups) unsalted butter,
softened

6 ounces semisweet chocolate, melted
and cooled
1 tablespoon eau-de-vie de
framboise

FOR THE MERINGUE

2 egg whites at room temperature
2 tablespoons granulated sugar
¼ cup confectioners' sugar, sifted

1 tablespoon eau-de-vie de
framboise

FOR THE DECORATION

meringue mushrooms (page 169)
chocolate leaves (page 171)

2 tablespoons almond paste tinted with
green food coloring

½ recipe raspberry sauce
(page 173), flavored with 4
tablespoons eau-de-vie de
framboise, or to taste

confectioners' sugar for sprinkling

Make the cake:

Preheat the oven to 425° F. Butter the jelly-roll pan and line it with wax paper, leaving a 2-inch overhang on each of the short ends. Butter the paper and dust it with flour, shaking out the excess.

In the large bowl of the upright mixer beat the egg yolks until smooth. Add 6 tablespoons of the granulated sugar, a little at a time, and beat the batter at medium speed for 3 to 4 minutes, or until creamy and light. Beat in the *framboise*. In another bowl with the hand-held mixer beat the egg whites with ⅛ teaspoon of the salt until frothy. Add the cream of tartar and beat the whites until they hold soft peaks. Add the remaining 2 tablespoons sugar, a little at a time, and beat the whites until they hold stiff peaks. Fold the whites into the batter gently but thoroughly. Sift the flour, the ¼ cup cocoa powder, and the remaining ⅛ teaspoon salt over the batter, one third at a time, and fold in each addition until the batter is smooth.

Pour the batter into the jelly-roll pan, spread it evenly with a spatula, and bake the cake in the middle of the oven for 8 to 10 minutes, or until it pulls away from the sides of the pan and a cake tester inserted in the center comes out clean. Dust the cake lightly with cocoa powder, cover it with wax paper, and let it cool to warm. Pull the edges of the wax paper away from the pan, invert the cake onto a baking sheet, and carefully peel off the paper. Dust the cake lightly with the remaining cocoa powder, cover it with wax paper, and roll it up (see illustrations page 30). Let the cake cool completely.

Make the chocolate buttercream: In the bowl of the upright mixer beat the egg yolks until light and creamy. In a small heavy saucepan combine the sugar with the water. Bring the mixture to a boil and cook it over moderate heat, stirring and washing down any sugar crystals clinging to the sides of the pan with the brush dipped in cold water until the syrup reaches the soft-ball stage, or the candy thermometer registers 238° F. With the mixer running, add the hot syrup to the yolks in a stream, beating, and beat the mixture until completely cool. Beat in the butter and the chocolate, a little at a time. Pour 2 cups of the buttercream into a bowl, beat in the *framboise*, and chill the buttercream, covered, until the cake is ready to be frosted. Transfer the remaining buttercream to a bowl and reserve it.

Make the meringue: In a bowl with the hand-held mixer beat the whites until they hold soft peaks. Add the granulated sugar and the confectioners' sugar, a little at a time, and beat the whites until they hold stiff peaks. Fold the meringue into the reserved buttercream, stir in the *framboise*, and blend the mixture until smooth.

To assemble the cake: Have ready the meringue mushrooms, chocolate leaves, and the colored almond paste.

Unroll the cake, spoon the ½ cup raspberry sauce over it, letting the cake absorb the sauce, and spread the buttercream-meringue filling evenly over the cake, leaving a 1-inch border on each of the long sides. Roll up the cake lengthwise.

Cut a 2-inch piece diagonally from each end of the cake and set the pieces aside. Transfer the cake to a serving tray and arrange the reserved end pieces on top of the cake to simulate sawed-off branches. Beat the chilled buttercream until smooth and with a spatula spread it over the cake. Gently pull the tines of a fork lengthwise over the buttercream to simulate bark and garnish the log with the meringue mushrooms and chocolate leaves. Force the green almond paste through a medium sieve and with the tip of a small knife attach it to the log around the mushrooms to simulate moss. Gently dust the log with sifted confectioners' sugar, simulating snow. Let the cake come to room temperature before serving. Cut the cake with a sharp serrated knife.

Photo on page 102.

CHOCOLATE RASPBERRY DOBOSTORTE

Yield:
one 8-inch-round
  9-layer cake,
  serving 12

Equipment:
three 8-inch round
  cake pans
hand-held and upright
  electric mixers
pastry brush
candy thermometer

One of the great Austrian specialties (although arriving via Hungary), Dobostorte is characterized by its caramel-coated top cake layer with individual slices marked while the caramel is still warm. The cake is made from sponge layers and is filled with chocolate buttercream and raspberry jam.

FOR THE CAKE LAYERS

6 large eggs, separated, the whites at room temperature
¾ cup plus 1 tablespoon sugar
1 teaspoon vanilla

1 cup cake flour (not self-rising)
¼ teaspoon plus pinch of salt
pinch of cream of tartar

FOR THE RASPBERRY FILLING

½ cup seedless raspberry jam
1 tablespoon eau-de-vie de framboise (raspberry brandy)

1 tablespoon fresh lemon juice, or to taste

1 recipe chocolate buttercream (page 64) made with 3 ounces semisweet chocolate, 2 ounces unsweetened chocolate, and 2 tablespoons eau-de-vie de framboise

½ cup toasted and skinned hazelnuts (for procedure page 174), chopped fine

FOR THE CARAMEL

1 cup sugar
¼ teaspoon cream of tartar

½ cup water

13 hazelnuts, toasted and skinned, for garnish

Make the cake layers:

Invert the cake pans and butter and flour the undersides. Preheat the oven to 350° F.

    In a large bowl with the hand-held mixer beat the egg yolks until thick and pale, beat in ½ cup of the sugar, and beat the mixture for 5 minutes. Beat in the vanilla. Sift the flour and the ¼ teaspoon salt together over the yolk mixture and fold them in gently but thoroughly. In another bowl with the hand-held mixer beat the whites with the pinch of salt until frothy, add the cream of tartar, and beat the whites until they hold soft peaks. Add the remaining 5 tablespoons sugar, a little at a time, beating, and beat the whites until they just hold stiff peaks. Stir one third of the whites into the batter and fold in the remaining whites gently but thoroughly.

    Spread a generous ½ cup of the batter with an icing spatula or a knife on each underside in an even layer and bake the cake layers on the same rack in

When the layers have cooled completely they may be stacked between sheets of wax paper, wrapped in plastic wrap, and chilled for 1 day. Remove the wax paper very carefully.

the middle of the oven for 7 to 9 minutes, or until pale golden. Let the cake layers cool for 2 minutes and loosen the edges with a thin-bladed knife. Transfer the layers to racks and let cool. Wipe the pans clean with paper towels and make 6 more layers in the same manner.

Make the raspberry filling:

In a small saucepan combine the jam, *eau-de-vie de framboise*, and the lemon juice, heat the mixture over moderately low heat, whisking, until smooth, and let cool to room temperature.

To assemble the cake:

Have ready the chocolate buttercream.

With a sharp knife trim the edges of the cake layers so that the layers are all the same size and shape, reserving the best layer, wrapped in plastic wrap, for the caramel top. Arrange one layer on a cake stand, using a small dab of the chocolate buttercream to anchor it to the stand, and spread it with 3 heaping tablespoons of the buttercream. Spread a second cake layer with 2 tablespoons of the raspberry filling, invert the layer, raspberry side down, onto the buttercream-spread layer, and spread the layer with 3 heaping tablespoons of buttercream. Continue to layer the remaining cake in the same manner. After spreading the eighth layer with the buttercream, spread the remaining buttercream around the sides of the cake. Chill the cake for 5 minutes to firm the buttercream slightly and press the chopped hazelnuts around the sides.

The cake may be prepared up to this point 2 days in advance and kept covered with an inverted bowl and chilled.

Make the caramel:

In a small saucepan combine the sugar, cream of tartar, and water, cook the mixture over moderate heat, stirring and washing down any sugar crystals clinging to the sides of the pan with the brush dipped in cold water until the sugar is dissolved, and bring the syrup to a boil. Boil the syrup, undisturbed, until it begins to turn a pale golden and swirl the pan gently until it is a golden brown caramel. While the syrup is boiling, put the reserved cake layer on a rack set over a few sheets of foil to protect the work surface and have ready a buttered knife. Pour enough of the caramel immediately over the cake layer to coat it with a thin layer, reserving the remaining caramel in the pan, and, working very quickly, draw the knife through the caramel glaze down to the cake, marking off 12 slices. (These lines decorate the cake and make it easier to slice without shattering the hardened caramel.) When the caramel has cooled completely, trim any caramel that has dripped around the edge with scissors.

Make the garnish:

Set a few sheets of foil over the work surface to protect it, invert a large sieve over the foil, and insert a wooden pick into the bottom of each whole hazelnut. Heat the reserved caramel over moderately low heat, swirling the pan, until it is melted. Dip the hazelnuts carefully into the caramel and insert the other end of the wooden picks into the sieve to allow the caramel to cool and harden. (Be very careful not to drip any caramel onto your hands or wear 2 pairs of rubber gloves to protect them from burns.) When the caramel-coated hazelnuts have cooled completely, press them onto the caramel-coated top cake layer, using some additional caramel, reheated, if necessary. Let the cake come to room temperature, arrange the caramel layer on top, and with a knife smooth the buttercream and chopped hazelnuts up around the edge of the the top layer.

PIES AND TARTS

*L*ife can be difficult, but a large wedge of chocolate cream or coconut custard pie, considered the ultimate indulgence, has a way of making everything just a little bit better. Perhaps this is a reason for the overwhelming popularity of pie in this country—not only as a dessert but also as a source for literary references. The expression, "As American as apple pie" rings true: Pie has always been and still is the favorite finale of memorable meals.

Making a truly great pie is considered an achievement; obtaining a flaky crust is considered "tricky," even difficult; and just exactly how long must you cook a custard or gel a chiffon filling? Successes are within everyone's grasp, however, and explicit instructions and, perhaps, just a little practice will help you achieve the "perfect" chocolate rum meringue pie, guaranteed to clinch your reputation as a top-notch baker.

A perfect fruit tart, a tender pastry shell displaying decoratively arranged fruits enhanced by a shiny glaze, does not have to be reserved for a special occasion. While pie is the overwhelming American favorite, its French relation, the tart, has always been standard dessert fare at luncheon, dinner, or at those other times, composed, for example, to offer an unexpected guest.

Tarts come in so many guises from simple and unadorned, almost rustic, to elegant and sophisticated. Either way, with the basic pairing of free-standing pastry shell and filling, the results will be delicious.

PIES

Pies are irresistible. They combine such elements as flaky crusts redolent with butter or with a satisfying crackle and crispness due to the addition of lard; fruit fillings with a magical balance of sweet and tart; custard fillings ranging from delicate and light to spicy and flavorful; light as air chiffon fillings; rich and creamy cream fillings; ethereal and always impressive meringue toppings; sweet and luscious nut fillings; and include single-serving deep-dish pies for the individualist in all of us.

A homemade pie shows that the baker cares. Not only has he risen to what is often considered a challenge, but because a pie is baked for some-one to make him happy (ask Billy Boy), it demonstrates a desire to please or even indulge. Eugene Field wrote, "The best of all physicians is apple pie and cheese." There must be a reason.

Pie can be simple and homey, like our Vanilla Cream Pie (page 86), easily prepared from ingredients on hand or from seasonal specialties as in our Black Raspberry Pie (page 78). It can be prepared from local ingredi-ents such as Key Lime Pie (page 85), ubiquitous, perhaps, in southern Florida, but an incredible treat throughout the rest of the country. Or a pie can be a fanciful combination but perfect marriage of ingredients as in our Eggnog Pie with Pecan Crust (page 90).

Any one of several pie doughs included here can be chosen to best enhance the pie filling or perhaps to best provide a contrast in texture or richness. Our lard pastry dough is used for Black Raspberry Pie. The crisp pastry holds up especially well to the juicy berry filling.

PIE DOUGHS

A baker's reputation is often built upon that person's ability to make light, flaky pie crusts. Although not difficult to achieve, an understanding of the proper techniques is necessary before you begin.

When blending the dough, handle it as little as possible. The heat from your fingertips will soften the shortening. This hampers the goal of small particles melting and blending with the flour while baking, creating tiny puffs of steam and resulting in a light, flaky, layered crust. You can use either your fingertips to combine the dry ingredients and butter, rub-bing the two together until the mixture resembles coarse meal, or you can cut the butter into the flour using two knives and a cutting motion to achieve small particles. Note that the shortening should be cold and ice

water is added to form a soft, moist, but not sticky dough. It is advisable to chill the dough for about 30 minutes to allow the gluten in the flour to relax and to make the dough more manageable.

Dust a work surface lightly with flour, and, using a very lightly dusted rolling pin, roll out the dough from the center outward to the edges in all directions forming a circle (or whatever the shape of the baking form) ⅛ inch thick (or whatever the recipe indicates) and larger than the form to ensure that it will fit with sufficient overhang.

To transfer the pastry to the pie plate, simply roll it loosely around the rolling pin, hold the rolling pin over the plate, and unroll the pastry over the plate, as shown in the illustrations below. With your fingertips or knuckles, gently press the pastry against the sides.

With a fork, prick the shell to prevent it from buckling or shrinking. Sometimes the shell is brushed with beaten egg white for especially juicy fillings. When baked, the egg white glaze helps prevent the liquid of the filling from being absorbed into the crust.

A pie usually has a decorative edge as opposed to being trimmed flush with the rim like many a tart shell is. After fitting the dough snugly into the pie plate, trim the edge with kitchen shears or a sharp knife to allow a ½-inch overhang. For a single-crust pie, form a decorative edge using one of the methods illustrated above. For a double-crust pie, drape the top layer of dough with a 1-inch overhang over the filling. Fold the top

Cutting in butter with fingertips/with two knives

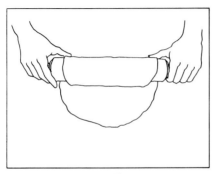
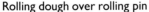

Rolling dough over rolling pin

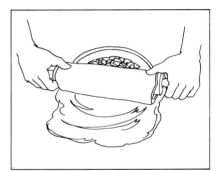

Rolling dough off rolling pin

Crimping dough for decorative edge: fluted edge; scalloped edge; rope edge

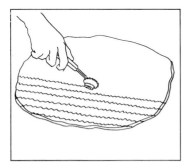 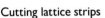 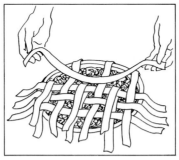 

Cutting lattice strips   Weaving lattice strips   A simple lattice crust, a decorative edge

crust under the bottom crust and crimp the edge decoratively. For a lattice crust, cut strips using a pastry wheel or sharp knife, and press the strips on in a lattice pattern (either woven or straight), firmly pressing the ends of the strips to the edge of the shell (see illustrations above).

Pie crusts can also be beautifully and amusingly garnished with pastry crust cutouts such as leaves scored to simulate veins and berries or a fruit, representative of the pie filling. The top crust, lattice crust, or pastry cutouts are sometimes brushed with an egg wash or sprinkled with sugar. An egg wash is a mixture of whole egg or egg yolk and water that is lightly beaten. When brushed on the top crust, it helps the pastry to brown and results in a shiny golden finish. When the egg is mixed with milk instead, it will result in a duller finish more suitable for a rustic look. Finally, steam vents may be cut in the top crust, allowing the steam from juicy fillings to escape, thereby preventing a possible soggy crust.

Recipes for crumb and nut crusts are included in this section. These crusts are particularly good with chiffon and cream fillings, their crunchy texture complementing the light creamy fillings. Our recipe for Apricot Chiffon Pie with a gingersnap crust is a splendid example.

FLAKY PIE PASTRY

Yield:
about 1 pound 2
  ounces dough
enough dough for 1
  double-crust 9-inch
  pie
or 2 single-crust
  9-inch pies

The dough may be
rolled out
immediately or it may
be kept, wrapped in
wax paper and chilled,
for up to 2 days. The
dough may be frozen,
wrapped in plastic
wrap and foil, for up
to 1 month.

2¼ cups all-purpose flour
½ teaspoon salt
½ stick (¼ cup) cold unsalted butter,
  cut into bits

½ cup cold vegetable shortening, cut
  into bits
¼ cup ice water

In a bowl combine the flour and salt, add the butter, and blend the mixture with your fingertips or two knives until it resembles coarse meal (see illustrations page 71). Add the shortening and blend the mixture until it resembles meal. Add the ice water, tossing the mixture with a fork, and adding more water if necessary to form a soft but not sticky dough. Shape the dough into a ball. If making a double-crust pie, or one with a lattice crust, divide the dough into 2 balls, one slightly larger than the other. If making 2 single-crust pies, halve the dough.

LARD PASTRY DOUGH

Yield:
about 1¼ pounds
  dough
enough dough for 1
  double-crust 9-inch
  pie
or 2 single-crust
  9-inch pies

2½ cups all-purpose flour
1 teaspoon salt
½ cup cold lard, cut into bits
1 egg yolk, beaten lightly

1 tablespoon fresh lemon juice
¼ to ½ cup ice water
1 stick (½ cup) unsalted butter, cut
  into bits

Into a bowl sift together the flour and the salt and blend in the lard with your fingertips or two knives until the mixture resembles coarse meal (see illustrations page 71). Add the egg yolk, lemon juice, and enough of the ice water to form a soft dough. Dust the dough with flour and roll it into a 16- by 7-inch rectangle. Dot the upper two thirds of the rectangle with the butter, pressing the butter gently into the dough, fold the lower third of the rectangle up to meet the center of the buttered portion, and fold the top of the rectangle over the bottom. Chill the dough, covered, for 30 minutes. Sprinkle the dough with flour, turn it seam side down so that an open side faces you, and roll it into a 16- by 7-inch rectangle. Fold the lower third of the dough to meet the center of the rectangle, fold the upper third to meet the center (so that both edges meet the center), and fold the top half over the bottom half. Chill the dough, covered, for 15 minutes. Roll out and fold the dough in the same manner one more time. Chill the dough, covered, for 30 minutes, or until firm. If making 2 single-crust pies, halve the dough.

The dough may be
kept, wrapped in wax
paper and chilled, for
up to 2 days. The
dough may be frozen,
wrapped in plastic
wrap and foil, for up
to 1 month.

OTHER CRUSTS

CHOCOLATE WAFER CRUMB CRUST

Yield:
one 9-inch pie crust

Equipment:
9-inch pie plate

2 cups chocolate wafer crumbs
⅓ cup sugar
¾ stick (6 tablespoons) unsalted
  butter, cut into bits and softened

2 egg whites
pinch of salt

Butter the pie plate lightly and preheat the oven to 300° F.

In a bowl combine the crumbs, sugar, and the butter and press the mixture onto the bottom and sides of the pie plate. Bake the shell on a baking sheet in the middle of the oven for 15 minutes and let it cool on a rack.

In a small bowl beat the egg whites with the salt until frothy and spoon them into the shell, spreading them gently with the back of a spoon to cover the bottom completely. Bake the shell on the baking sheet in the middle of the oven for 5 minutes and let it cool on a rack.

GRAHAM CRACKER CRUST

Yield:
one 9-inch pie crust

Equipment:
9-inch pie plate

1½ cups graham cracker crumbs
  (about 11 crackers)
¼ cup sugar if desired

½ stick (¼ cup) unsalted butter,
  melted

Preheat the oven to 350° F.

In a bowl combine the crumbs, the sugar if desired, and the butter and press the mixture evenly onto the bottom and sides of the pie plate. Bake the shell on a baking sheet in the lower third of the oven for 5 minutes. Let the shell cool on a rack.

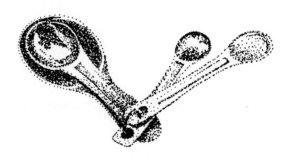

NUT CRUST

Yield:
one 9-inch pie crust

Equipment:
9-inch pie plate

2 cups pecans or toasted and skins removed hazelnuts (for procedure page 174)

1/3 cup sugar
3 tablespoons unsalted butter, melted

Preheat the oven to 350° F.

In a blender pulverize the nuts and transfer them to a bowl. Combine the nuts well with the sugar and blend in the melted butter. Press the mixture evenly onto the bottom and sides of the pie plate and chill the shell for 30 minutes. Bake the shell on a baking sheet in the middle of the oven for 12 to 15 minutes, or until lightly browned around the edges. Let the shell cool on a rack.

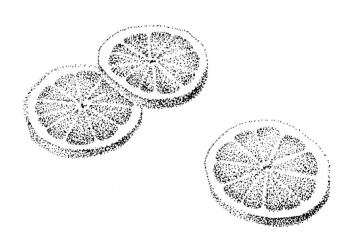

FRUIT PIES

Fresh ripe fruits and seasoning to enhance each fruit's flavor are the important things to remember for a fruit filling. Apples, berries, and pears are suggested here.

Deep-dish pies are made without bottom crusts in deep baking pans. Because of the greater amount of fruit, they are especially juicy and flavorful. We have included an interesting recipe for individual deep-dish pies of cranberries and apples prepared in soufflé cups or ramekins and topped with a pastry crust. A wonderful pie topping is a streusel or crumb one and we use it to enhance the flavor of fresh peaches in our Streusel Peach Pie (page 79).

APPLE PIE

Yield:
one 9-inch pie

Equipment:
deep 9-inch pie plate

The traditional American favorite with an especially spicy and flavorful filling that includes golden raisins. Among the best varieties of apples to use for baking are: Greenings, Pippins, Golden Delicious, McIntosh, Rome Beauties, Jonathans, Staymans, Granny Smiths, and Winesaps.

1 recipe flaky pie pastry (page 73), divided into 2 balls, one slightly larger than the other

FOR THE FILLING

6 large Greening apples, peeled, cored, and thinly sliced
1 cup granulated sugar
2 tablespoons all-purpose flour
½ teaspoon cinnamon

½ teaspoon freshly grated nutmeg
pinch of salt
½ teaspoon grated lemon rind, or to taste
¾ cup golden raisins

1½ cups confectioners' sugar
2 tablespoons water
¼ teaspoon vanilla
heavy cream as an accompaniment if desired

vanilla ice cream as an accompaniment if desired

On a floured surface roll out the larger ball of dough ¹/₁₆ inch thick. Drape the dough over the rolling pin, unroll it over the plate, and fit it into the plate (see illustrations page 71). Trim the edge to form a ½-inch overhang. Chill the shell and remaining dough while preparing the filling.

Preheat the oven to 350° F.

Make the filling:

Toss the apples with the granulated sugar, 1 tablespoon of the flour, the cinnamon, nutmeg, salt, and the lemon rind. Toss the raisins with the remaining 1 tablespoon flour.

Alternate layers of the apple mixture and the floured raisins in the chilled pie shell. Roll out the remaining ball of dough ¹/₁₆ inch thick on the floured surface and drape it over the filling, trimming it to a ½-inch overhang. Fold the top crust under the bottom crust and crimp the edges decoratively (see illustrations page 72). Make decorative slits in the top crust for steam vents. Bake the pie in middle of the oven for 60 to 70 minutes, or until the apples are tender and the crust is golden. Let the pie cool on a rack completely.

In a small bowl combine the confectioners' sugar, water, and the vanilla and mix until smooth. Spread the top crust with the glaze. The pie can be served slightly warm or at room temperature with heavy cream or ice cream as an accompaniment if desired.

STRAWBERRY RHUBARB PIE

Yield:
one 9-inch pie

1 recipe flaky pie pastry (page 73), divided into 2 balls, one slightly larger than the other

Equipment:
9-inch pie plate
pastry brush

FOR THE FILLING

2 cups (about 1 pint) hulled, sliced strawberries

1 cup sugar, or to taste, plus sugar for sprinkling the top crust

2 tablespoons cornstarch dissolved in 1 tablespoon cold water

8 ounces rhubarb, trimmed and cut into ¾-inch pieces to measure 2 cups

½ teaspoon grated lemon rind, or to taste

1 teaspoon fresh lemon juice

2 tablespoons unsalted butter, cut into bits

Chill the balls of dough, covered, for 1 hour. On a floured surface roll the larger ball into an 11-inch round. Drape the dough over the rolling pin, unroll it over the pie plate, and fit it into the plate (see illustrations page 71). Trim the edge to form a ½-inch overhang. Reserve the smaller ball, covered and chilled.

Make the filling: In a bowl combine the strawberries and the 1 cup sugar, let the mixture stand for 20 minutes, and stir in the cornstarch mixture. Add the rhubarb, lemon rind, and lemon juice and spoon the mixture into the pie shell. Dot the mixture with the butter.

Preheat the oven to 400° F.

On the floured surface roll the reserved ball of dough into a 10-inch round and drape the top crust over the filling. Trim the top crust, leaving a ½-inch overhang, fold it under the bottom crust to seal the pie, and crimp the edge decoratively (see illustrations page 72). Sprinkle the top of the pie with sugar and make decorative slits in the crust for steam vents. Bake in the middle of the oven for 40 to 50 minutes, or until the crust is golden. Let the pie cool on a rack.

BLACK RASPBERRY PIE

Yield:
one 9-inch pie

Equipment:
9-inch pie plate
baking sheet

Black raspberries are simply a slightly less sweet variety of red raspberries. This recipe also calls for plump, juicy, full-flavored blackberries, sweet but with a wonderful tartness, which are available wild or cultivated. Varieties of the blackberry that could be substituted are boysenberries, loganberries, and olallieberries.

1 recipe lard pastry dough (page 73), divided into 2 balls, one slightly larger than the other

FOR THE FILLING

1 cup sugar
3 to 4 tablespoons all-purpose flour
¼ teaspoon grated lemon rind
1 pint black raspberries, picked over

1½ cups blackberries, picked over
1 tablespoon fresh lemon juice
1 tablespoon unsalted butter, cut into bits

vanilla ice cream as an accompaniment if desired

Make the filling:

In a bowl combine well the sugar, 3 tablespoons of the flour, and the lemon rind. Add the black raspberries, the blackberries, and the lemon juice and toss the berries to coat them with the mixture. Add up to 1 tablespoon more flour if the berries are very juicy.

Preheat the oven to 425° F.

On a floured surface roll out the larger ball of dough ⅛ inch thick. Drape the dough over the rolling pin, unroll it over the pie plate, and fit it into the plate (see illustrations page 71). Trim the edge to form a ½-inch overhang. Spread the filling in the shell and dot it with the butter. Roll out the remaining ball of dough ⅛ inch thick on the floured surface and drape it over the filling. Trim the top crust, leaving a 1-inch overhang, and fold it under the bottom crust. Crimp the edge decoratively (see illustrations page 72) and make slits in the top crust for steam vents. Bake on the baking sheet in the lower third of the oven for 10 minutes. Reduce the oven temperature to 375° F. and bake the pie for 40 to 50 minutes more, or until the crust is golden and the filling is bubbly. Transfer to a rack and let cool. Serve the pie warm or at room temperature with the ice cream if desired.

STREUSEL PEACH PIE

Yield:
one 11-inch pie

Equipment:
11-inch pie plate, 1½
  inches deep
pastry brush

*1 recipe pâte brisée (page 116),
  rolled ⅛ inch thick, transferred to
  pie plate, and fitted in (see
  illustrations page 71)*

FOR THE STREUSEL
*⅔ cup firmly packed light brown
  sugar
3 tablespoons all-purpose flour*

*3 pounds peaches, peeled (for
  procedure page 174), pitted, and
  sliced
1 tablespoon fresh lemon juice*

*raw rice or dried beans for weighting
  the shell
1 egg white, beaten lightly*

*1 teaspoon cinnamon
½ stick (¼ cup) cold unsalted butter,
  cut into bits*

Trim the edge of the dough to leave a ½-inch overhang. Crimp the edge of the shell decoratively (see illustrations page 72). Prick the bottom of the shell with a fork and chill for 30 minutes.

Preheat the oven to 425° F.

Line, weight, and blind-bake the shell (see illustrations page 115) in the lower third of the oven for 15 minutes. Carefully remove the rice and paper and bake the shell for 15 minutes. Brush the bottom and sides with the egg white and bake the shell for 5 minutes more, or until golden. Transfer the shell to a rack and let cool.

Make the streusel: In a small bowl combine the brown sugar, flour, and the cinnamon. Blend in the butter until the mixture resembles coarse meal. Sprinkle one third of the streusel into the bottom of the shell. Arrange half the peach slices, overlapping them slightly, in concentric circles over the streusel. Sprinkle the slices with half the remaining streusel and drizzle with some of the lemon juice. Top the streusel with the remaining slices, arranging them in the same manner, drizzle the slices with the remaining lemon juice, and sprinkle the remaining streusel over them.

Reduce the oven temperature to 375° F. Bake the pie in the middle of the oven for 45 to 55 minutes, or until the filling is bubbling and the peaches are tender. Transfer the pie to a rack to cool. Serve the pie at room temperature.

Photo on page 103.

CRANBERRY MAPLE PEAR PIE

Yield:
one 9-inch pie

Equipment:
9-inch pie plate
fluted pastry wheel
cardboard template in
the shape of a maple
leaf, about 3 inches
long and 2½ inches
wide

*1 recipe flaky pie pastry (page 73)
divided into 2 balls, one larger than
the other; the larger ball rolled ⅛
inch thick, transferred to pie plate,
and fitted in (see illustrations page
71)*
*3 cups (a 12-ounce bag) fresh or
frozen cranberries, picked over*

1 cup maple syrup
*1 pound pears, peeled, cored, and cut
into ¼-inch pieces*
*4½ teaspoons cornstarch dissolved in 2
tablespoons cold water*

In a saucepan combine the cranberries, syrup, and pears, bring the mixture to a boil, and simmer it, stirring occasionally, for 3 to 4 minutes, or until the cranberries have popped. Stir the cornstarch mixture, stir it into the cranberry mixture, and simmer the mixture, stirring, for 1 minute, or until thickened. Transfer the mixture to a bowl and let it cool.

Trim off the excess dough from the sides of the pie shell, leaving a 1-inch overhang and reserving the scraps. Fold the overhang over the rim and crimp the edges decoratively (see illustrations page 72). Prick the bottom of the shell with a fork and chill the shell for 30 minutes. Wrap the reserved scraps in plastic and chill while cutting the dough for the lattice crust.

On a floured surface roll out the other ball of dough ⅛ inch thick and with the pastry wheel or a sharp knife cut out ½-inch strips of the dough. Transfer the strips to a baking sheet and chill them for 10 minutes, or until they are just firm enough to work with. (If the strips get too cold they will become brittle and break.)

On the lightly floured surface roll out the reserved scraps ⅛ inch thick and freeze the dough on a small baking sheet for 5 minutes, or until firm. Using the template cut out 2 maple leaves from the dough with scissors or a sharp knife and chill them on a flat surface.

Preheat the oven to 425° F.

Spoon the filling into the shell, spreading it evenly, and arrange the lattice strips on top (see illustrations page 72), twisting each strip corkscrew fashion. Trim the ends of the strips flush with the overhang of the shell, pressing them onto the shell, turn up the overhanging dough, and crimp the edge decoratively. Score the pastry maple leaves decoratively with a knife, arrange them on the lattice, and bake the pie in the upper third of the oven for 40 to 45 minutes, or until the pastry is golden and the filling is bubbling. Let the pie cool on a rack.

Photo on page 104.

The cranberry mixture may be made up to 1 day in advance and kept covered and chilled.

The pie may be made up to 1 day in advance and kept, covered loosely, in a cool, dry place. If making the pie 1 day in advance reheat it in a preheated 350° F. oven for 10 to 15 minutes to crisp the crust.

INDIVIDUAL CRANBERRY APPLE DEEP-DISH PIES

Yield:
twelve 1-cup
  individual pies

Equipment:
twelve 1-cup soufflé
  cups or ramekins

Individual deep-dish pies are a wonderful idea and can be frozen with such excellent results that they should be prepared to take advantage of seasonal fruits such as peaches and plums. These extremely homey desserts can be dressed up with pastry cutouts for a slightly fancier presentation.

1 recipe flaky pie pastry (page 73)

FOR THE FILLING
3 large eggs
2 cups sugar, or to taste
6 tablespoons all-purpose flour
18 ounces (1½ packages) cranberries (fresh or frozen), picked over and chopped coarse
2 pounds apples (about 5 medium-large), peeled, cored, and chopped coarse

½ cup coarsely chopped walnuts
½ cup raisins
¼ cup fresh orange juice
1 teaspoon grated orange rind

Preheat the oven to 450° F.

Make the filling:
  In a bowl beat the eggs with the sugar until blended well. Gradually add the flour by tablespoons and beat well. Add the cranberries, apples, walnuts, raisins, orange juice, and the rind and toss gently. Divide the filling among the individual cups.

  On a lightly floured board roll out the dough in a rectangle ⅛ inch thick. Cut out 12 rounds ⅓ inch larger than the soufflé cups. Put a pastry round on top of each cup and, pressing with the tines of a fork, seal the pastry to the rim of the cup.

  Place the cups on a baking sheet and bake the pies in the middle of the oven for 15 minutes. Reduce the temperature to 400° F. and bake the pies for 10 minutes more, or until the crusts are golden. Serve warm or cool.

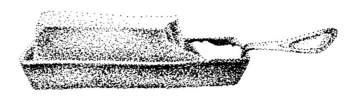

CUSTARD AND CREAM PIES

Custard and cream pies, while basically composed of the same ingredients, use different cooking methods in combining them. The custard mixture bakes in the oven while the cream filling is cooked on top of the stove, thickened with cornstarch, and is poured into a prebaked shell. One exception is our recipe for Coconut Custard Pie (page 84). There, the custard and shell are cooked separately and the "slipped custard" method is employed to assemble the two.

A custard filling should be set but still slightly quivery when removed from the oven as it will continue baking while cooling. You want to be careful not to overbake or bake a custard filling at too high a temperature, as it will become too firm and dense. So check your oven with an oven thermometer if you suspect that your oven temperature may not be accurate.

Cream fillings must be stirred constantly while cooking over moderate heat. This will prevent undesirable lumps from forming and reduce the risk of scorching the cream. Like the custard filling, the cream filling will set up while chilling in the prepared pie shell.

Custard pies, though simple and often unassuming in appearance, are truly beloved. As the recipes included in our custard section indicate, these are the pies that have been embraced by Americans as part of their holiday feasts or family celebrations. What Thanksgiving dinner is considered complete without a pecan pumpkin pie? And coconut custard has always been and remains a favorite at family gatherings.

Whether or not they admit it, almost everyone loves cream pies. Rich but not too rich, sweet but not too sweet, a creamy vanilla-flavored filling is poured into a flaky shell and the combination is superb. Even better when a layer of banana slices is added or when the filling is chocolate or butterscotch flavored and served in a crumb crust. We have included recipes for all of them.

PECAN PUMPKIN PIE

Yield:
one 9-inch pie

Equipment:
9-inch pie plate

½ recipe flaky pie pastry (page 73)

FOR THE PUMPKIN LAYER
¾ cup canned pumpkin purée
*2 tablespoons firmly packed light
    brown sugar*
1 large egg, beaten lightly

2 tablespoons sour cream
⅛ teaspoon cinnamon
⅛ teaspoon freshly grated nutmeg

FOR THE PECAN LAYER
¾ cup light corn syrup
*½ cup firmly packed light brown
    sugar*
3 large eggs, beaten lightly
*3 tablespoons unsalted butter, melted
    and cooled*

2 teaspoons vanilla
¼ teaspoon freshly grated lemon rind
1½ teaspoons fresh lemon juice
¼ teaspoon salt
1⅓ cups pecans

Preheat the oven to 425° F.

On a lightly floured surface roll out the dough ⅛ inch thick. Drape the dough over the rolling pin, unroll it over the plate, and fit it into the plate (see illustrations page 71). Trim the edge to form a ½-inch overhang. Crimp the edges decoratively (see illustrations page 72). Chill the shell while making the filling layers.

Make the pumpkin layer:

In a small bowl whisk together the pumpkin purée, brown sugar, egg, sour cream, cinnamon, and the nutmeg until the mixture is smooth.

Make the pecan layer:

In a small bowl combine well the corn syrup, brown sugar, eggs, butter, vanilla, rind, lemon juice, and the salt and stir in the pecans.

The pie may be made 1 day in advance and kept, covered loosely and chilled. If making the pie in advance, reheat it in a preheated 350° F. oven for 10 to 15 minutes, or until the crust is crisp.

Spread the pumpkin mixture evenly in the chilled pie shell and carefully spoon the pecan mixture over it. Bake the pie in the upper third of the oven for 20 minutes, reduce the heat to 350° F., and bake the pie for 20 to 30 minutes more, or until the filling is puffed slightly. (The center will appear to be not quite set.) Let the pie cool on a rack.

Photo on page 104.

COCONUT CUSTARD PIE

Yield:
one 9-inch pie

Equipment:
two 9-inch non-stick
  pie plates
food processor fitted
  with steel blade
cheesecloth
larger pan for
  waterbath

The custard and shell in this recipe are cooked separately to prevent the shell from becoming soggy—an unfortunate but not uncommon occurrence when the two are baked together. After cooling, the custard is simply slipped from the pie plate into the shell (explaining the name of this technique, "slipped custard"), and the pie can then sit at room temperature for several hours, or it can be chilled.

If you substitute sweetened flaked coconut for the fresh coconut, be sure to eliminate or reduce the sugar measurement in the custard.

*½ recipe flaky pie pastry (page 73),
  rolled ⅛ inch thick, transferred to
  pie plate, and fitted in (see
  illustrations page 71)*

*raw rice or dried beans for weighting
  the shell*

FOR THE FILLING

*2½ cups half-and-half
3 cups grated fresh coconut (for
  procedure page 174), or sweetened
  flaked coconut*

*4 large eggs
½ cup sugar
2 teaspoons vanilla
pinch of salt*

*lightly whipped cream for garnish if
  desired*

*½ cup grated coconut, toasted, for
  garnish if desired*

Trim the edge of the shell, leaving a ½-inch overhang. Crimp the edge of the shell decoratively (see illustrations page 72). Prick the dough with a fork and chill it for 30 minutes.

Preheat the oven to 400° F.

Line, weight, and blind-bake the shell (see instructions page 115) in the lower third of the oven for 15 minutes. Remove the wax paper and rice. Reduce the oven temperature to 375° F. and bake the shell for 10 minutes more, or until golden. Transfer the shell to a rack and let it cool.

Reduce the oven temperature to 350° F. and butter the second pie plate.

Make the filling:

In a saucepan bring the half-and-half to a simmer, stir in 2 cups of the fresh coconut, and let the mixture stand for 20 minutes, or until it is room temperature. Transfer the coconut milk to the food processor and blend it for 1 minute. Strain the mixture through a sieve lined with the cheesecloth, squeezing the cheesecloth to extract all of the liquid, and add the eggs, sugar, vanilla, and salt. Stir in the remaining 1 cup coconut and pour the custard into the pie plate. Put the pie plate in the larger pan, add enough hot water to the pan to come halfway up the sides of the plate, and bake in the middle of the oven for for 30 to 35 minutes, or until the edges of the custard are set. (The center of the custard will still be a bit loose but will set as it cools in the pan.) Transfer the pie plate to a rack and let it cool to room temperature. Using a plastic or rubber spatula, gently slide the custard into the shell and garnish the top of the pie with the whipped cream and toasted coconut, if desired.

KEY LIME PIE

Yield:
one 9-inch pie

Equipment:
9-inch pie plate
hand-held electric
   mixer

Key limes are indigenous to the Florida Keys and to parts of the Caribbean. If you are not fortunate enough to be able to obtain Key limes in Florida or from a particularly good specialty produce market, bottled Key lime juice may be substituted, or a combination of freshly squeezed lemon juice and Tahiti or Persian lime juice. Key lime pies can also be made with graham cracker crusts and may be topped with either sweetened whipped cream or meringue.

1 recipe pâte brisée *(page 116),
   rolled into an 11-inch round ⅛ inch
   thick, transferred to pie plate, and
   fitted in (see illustrations page 71)*

*raw rice or dried beans for weighting
   the shell*

FOR THE FILLING
3 egg yolks
*½ cup freshly squeezed or bottled Key
   lime juice*
1 teaspoon grated lime rind

*one 15-ounce can sweetened condensed
   milk*
*drop or two of green food coloring if
   desired*

1 cup well-chilled heavy cream

3 tablespoons confectioners' sugar

Press the dough firmly into the pan, leaving a ½-inch overhang, and crimp the edges decoratively (see illustrations page 72). Prick the bottom of the shell with a fork and chill the shell for 30 minutes.

Preheat the oven to 400° F.

Line, weight, and blind-bake the shell (see illustrations page 115) in the lower third of the oven for 10 minutes. Remove the rice and paper and bake the shell for 10 to 15 minutes more, or until lightly colored. Transfer the shell to a rack and let it cool.

Make the filling:

In a bowl with the mixer beat the egg yolks until light and lemon colored and add the lime juice and lime rind. Beat in the condensed milk and enough of the food coloring to attain a natural lime tint if desired. Pour the custard into the baked pie shell.

Reduce the oven temperature to 350° F.

Bake the pie in the middle of the oven for about 15 minutes. Transfer the pie to a rack and let it cool completely.

In a well-chilled bowl with the mixer beat the heavy cream until it holds soft peaks. Sift the confectioners' sugar over it and continue to beat the cream until it holds almost stiff peaks.

Spread the whipped cream with a metal spatula over the cooled pie filling, making decorative peaks. Serve the pie well chilled.

Variation:

KEY LIME PIE WITH MERINGUE TOPPING: Beat 4 egg whites until stiff but not dry and gradually beat in ½ cup superfine granulated sugar and 1 teaspoon lime juice. Spread the meringue generously over the filling, swirling it into irregular decorative peaks. Bake in a preheated 350° F. oven for about 15 minutes, or until the meringue is lightly browned.

VANILLA CREAM PIE

Yield:
one 9-inch pie

Equipment:
9-inch pie plate

The title of this recipe is a slight misnomer as the filling contains no cream. However, the consistency of the cornstarch-thickened filling is smooth and creamy enough to merit the name. For an even richer filling increase the amount of butter to six tablespoons.

½ recipe flaky pie pastry (page 73), rolled ⅛ inch thick, transferred to pie plate, and fitted in (see illustrations page 71)

raw rice or dried beans for weighting the shell

FOR THE FILLING

¾ cup sugar
⅓ cup cornstarch
¼ teaspoon salt
2¾ cups milk

4 egg yolks, beaten lightly
3 tablespoons unsalted butter
2½ teaspoons vanilla

Trim the dough, leaving a ½-inch overhang. Crimp the edge of the shell decoratively (see illustrations page 72). Prick the bottom of the shell with a fork and chill the shell for 30 minutes.

Preheat the oven to 400° F.

Line, weight, and blind-bake the shell (see illustrations page 115) in the lower third of the oven for 15 minutes. Carefully remove the rice and paper. Reduce the oven temperature to 375° F. and bake the shell for 10 minutes or until golden. Transfer the shell to a rack and let it cool.

Make the filling:

In saucepan but off the heat whisk together the sugar, cornstarch, and salt. Add the milk in a very slow stream, whisking constantly, whisk in the egg yolks gradually, and combine the filling well. Cook the filling over moderate heat, whisking constantly, until it reaches a full boil. Reduce the heat to low and, continuing to stir constantly, cook for 4 minutes. Remove the pan from the heat and stir in the butter and vanilla. Transfer the mixture to a bowl and cover the surface of the filling directly with a large round of buttered plastic wrap or wax paper to prevent a skin from forming. Let the filling cool to room temperature.

Pour the filling into the cooled pie shell and refrigerate the pie until completely set.

Variations:

CHOCOLATE CREAM PIE: Melt 3 ounces unsweetened chocolate and let cool. Add the melted chocolate to the milk and combine thoroughly. Proceed with the recipe as directed and pour the chocolate filling into a baked cooled graham cracker crust (page 74). For a Double Chocolate Cream Pie replace the graham cracker crust with a baked cooled chocolate wafer crumb crust (page 74).

BANANA CREAM PIE: Peel 3 bananas and cut them into ¼-inch slices. Arrange the slices in the bottom of the baked cooled pie shell and cover them with the cooled vanilla cream filling.

BUTTERSCOTCH CREAM PIE: Substitute 1 cup firmly packed dark brown sugar for the sugar, being careful to break up any lumps when combining it with the cornstarch and the salt. Reduce the amount of vanilla to 2 teaspoons. Proceed as directed above and pour the cooled filling into a baked cooled graham cracker crust (page 74).

HAZELNUT PRALINE CREAM PIE: Reduce the amount of sugar to ½ cup and substitute 2½ teaspoons Frangelico (hazelnut liqueur), or to taste, for the vanilla. When incorporating the butter and Frangelico, fold in ½ cup finely ground hazelnut praline (page 167). Let the filling cool and pour it into a baked cooled nut crust (page 75) made with hazelnuts.

CHIFFON AND MERINGUE PIES

As chiffon is a fabric characterized by its gossamer, light nature, so its namesake shares those same ethereal qualities. Chiffon pies have a delicate texture, a sheerness achieved by the addition of whipped egg whites or heavy cream to the filling. Gelatin is often added, providing support for the airy structure.

The fillings are enhanced by slightly crunchy nut or crumb crusts, which also have the advantage of absorbing moisture less quickly from the fillings. Our Pumpkin Chiffon Pie (page 89) is the perfect solution when a traditional spicy and seasonal Thanksgiving dessert is required but an airier, less heavy one is desired. Likewise, Eggnog Pie with Pecan Crust (page 90) is a wonderful and authentic holiday dessert but lighter than the norm.

Meringue pies are also ethereal, but in a different way. They are topped with a tender egg white and sugar combination, stiffly beaten and lightly browned, or are made with a baked meringue shell, crisp but tender. Not only do we include a recipe for chocolate rum meringue or "angel" pie, but we offer Cranberry Meringue Pie (page 93), exquisite not only in its combination of flavors but also in its appearance. This pie is guaranteed to become a Christmas favorite.

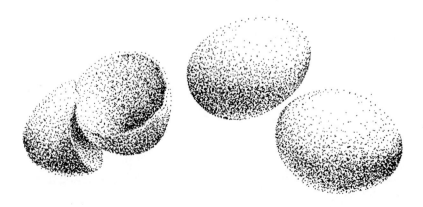

PUMPKIN CHIFFON PIE

Yield:
one 9½-inch pie

Equipment:
9½-inch pie plate
hand-held electric
  mixer
pastry bag fitted with
  decorative tip

1 recipe pâte brisée *(page 116),
  substituting 2 teaspoons sugar for
  the salt; rolled ⅛ inch thick,
  transferred to pie plate, and fitted
  in (see illustrations page 71)*

*raw rice or dried beans for weighting
  the shell*

FOR THE FILLING
*1 cup firmly packed dark brown sugar
5 large eggs, separated, at room
  temperature
1 teaspoon cinnamon
½ teaspoon freshly grated nutmeg
¼ teaspoon ground ginger*

*⅛ teaspoon ground allspice
2 cups canned pumpkin purée
½ cup heavy cream
5 tablespoons unsalted butter, melted
pinch of salt
¼ cup granulated sugar*

*sweetened whipped cream flavored
  with dark rum for garnish*

*12 candied pecan halves (page 168)
  for garnish*

Trim the excess dough from the sides of the shell, leaving a 1-inch over-hang, fold the overhang over the rim, pressing it onto the sides of the shell, and crimp the edges decoratively (see illustrations page 72). Prick the bottom of the shell with a fork and chill the shell for 1 hour.

Preheat the oven to 400° F.

Line, weight, and blind-bake the shell (see illustrations page 115) in the middle of the oven for 10 minutes. Carefully remove the rice and paper and bake the shell for 10 to 15 minutes more, or until lightly colored. Let cool on a rack.

Reduce the oven temperature to 375° F.

Make the filling: In a bowl combine well the brown sugar, egg yolks, cinnamon, nutmeg, ginger, and allspice. In a large bowl combine the pumpkin purée, heavy cream, and butter, add the sugar mixture, and mix well. In another large bowl with the mixer beat the egg whites with the salt until they hold soft peaks. Sprinkle in the granulated sugar, one tablespoon at a time, beating, and continue to beat the whites until they hold stiff peaks. Fold the whites into the pumpkin mixture gently but thoroughly. Pour the filling into the shell.

Bake the pie in the middle of the oven for 40 to 45 minutes, or until the filling is puffed and set. Let cool on a rack. With the pastry bag garnish the pie with a border of whipped cream rosettes separated by candied pecan halves. (For detailed instructions on working with a pastry bag and piping rosettes, see page 14.) Sprinkle 4 candied pecan halves, chopped, in the center of the pie and top them with a candied pecan half.

EGGNOG PIE WITH PECAN CRUST

Yield:
one 9½-inch pie

Equipment:
9½-inch pie plate
hand-held electric
  mixer
pastry bag fitted with
  decorative tip

This glorious chiffon pie is flavored with both brandy and rum, resulting in a rich egg custard filling that is then lightened with whipped heavy cream and beaten egg whites. The pie has a pecan crust and is garnished with both rum-flavored whipped cream and chocolate curls. To make the eggnog flavoring even more authentic, dust the pie with nutmeg.

1 prebaked nut crust (page 75), made with 2½ cups ground pecans and an additional tablespoon unsalted butter

FOR THE FILLING
1½ tablespoons unflavored gelatin
3 tablespoons brandy
4 large eggs, separated, at room temperature
⅓ cup granulated sugar
1⅓ cups milk, scalded

¼ cup dark rum
1½ teaspoons vanilla
pinch of salt
¾ cup well-chilled heavy cream, lightly whipped

FOR THE TOPPING
1 cup well-chilled heavy cream
2 to 3 tablespoons sifted confectioners' sugar

1 to 2 tablespoons dark rum, or to taste

chocolate curls (page 170) for garnish

Make the filling:

In a small bowl sprinkle the gelatin over the brandy to soften for 10 minutes. In a bowl with the mixer beat the egg yolks with the sugar until the mixture falls in a ribbon when the beater is lifted (see illustration page 10). Add the scalded milk in a stream, stirring. Pour the mixture into a heavy saucepan and cook it over moderately low heat, stirring, with a wooden spoon, until it is thick enough to coat the spoon, but do not let it boil. Remove the pan from the heat and add the softened gelatin, rum, and vanilla, stirring until the gelatin is dissolved. Transfer the custard to a bowl set over a larger bowl of ice and cold water and let it cool, stirring occasionally, but do not let it set.

In a large bowl with the mixer beat the egg whites with the salt until they hold stiff peaks. Fold in the whipped heavy cream and the custard gently but thoroughly.

Pour enough of the filling into the prepared shell to fill the shell to the top and chill the pie for 20 minutes, or until the filling is set. Transfer the remaining filling to the shell, mounding it over the top, and chill the pie for 20 minutes more, or until set.

Make the topping:

In a chilled bowl with the mixer beat the heavy cream with the confectioners' sugar and the rum until it holds soft peaks.

Spread the whipped cream over the pie, mounding it slightly and re-serving a small amount for garnish. With the pastry bag pipe the reserved whipped cream decoratively around the edge of the pie and decorate the center and sides with the chocolate curls. Sprinkle bits of broken chocolate curls over the whipped cream and chill the pie. Remove the pie from the refrigerator at least 30 minutes before serving.

APRICOT CHIFFON PIE WITH GINGERSNAP CRUST

Yield:
one 9-inch pie

Equipment:
9-inch pie plate
food processor fitted
  with steel blade
hand-held electric
  mixer

FOR THE SHELL
1⅓ cups gingersnap crumbs
3 tablespoons confectioners' sugar
½ stick (¼ cup) unsalted butter,
  melted and cooled

FOR THE FILLING
1½ teaspoons unflavored gelatin
1 tablespoon fresh lime juice
¾ cup dried apricots
1 cup water
½ cup plus 3 tablespoons granulated
  sugar

½ cup apple juice
½ cup sour cream
3 egg whites at room temperature
pinch of salt
pinch of cream of tartar

1 gingersnap, crumbled, for garnish

Preheat the oven to 400° F.

Make the shell: In a bowl combine the gingersnap crumbs, the confectioners' sugar, and the butter. Press the mixture into the pie plate and bake it in the middle of the oven for 8 minutes. Let the shell cool on a rack.

Make the filling: In a small bowl sprinkle the gelatin over the lime juice and let it soften for 10 minutes. In a saucepan combine the apricots, water, and the ½ cup sugar, bring the mixture to a boil over moderate heat, and simmer it for 20 minutes. In the food processor purée the mixture, transfer it to a large bowl, and add the gelatin mixture, stirring until the gelatin is dissolved. Stir in the apple juice and let the mixture cool. Fold in the sour cream. In a bowl with the mixer beat the egg whites with the salt and the cream of tartar until frothy. Add the remaining 3 tablespoons sugar, one teaspoon at a time, beating, and beat the whites until they hold soft peaks. Fold the egg whites into the apricot mixture gently but thoroughly.

Turn the filling into the shell and chill the pie for at least 6 hours. Just before serving, garnish the pie with the crumbled gingersnap.

CHOCOLATE RUM MERINGUE PIE

Yield:
one 9-inch pie

Equipment:
9-inch metal pie plate
hand-held electric
   mixer

A pie made with a meringue shell is often called an angel pie. The shell can be baked ahead and kept crisp in a turned-off oven overnight. The shell can even be frozen, tightly wrapped. Fill the shell at least one hour before serving, which will allow the meringue to soften slightly.

FOR THE MERINGUE SHELL

2 egg whites at room temperature
pinch of salt
¼ teaspoon cream of tartar

½ cup superfine granulated sugar
½ teaspoon vanilla

FOR THE FILLING

6 ounces semisweet chocolate, chopped
   coarse
4 egg whites at room temperature
pinch of salt

¼ teaspoon cream of tartar
1 cup well-chilled heavy cream
2 tablespoons dark rum

sweetened whipped heavy cream for garnish

Butter the pie pan well and preheat the oven to 275° F.

Make the meringue shell:

   In a bowl with the mixer beat the egg whites with the salt until foamy, add the cream of tartar, and beat the whites until they hold soft peaks. Add the superfine sugar, one tablespoon at a time, and beat the meringue until it holds very stiff peaks. Beat in the vanilla. Spoon the meringue into the pie plate, forming the sides of the shell with the back of the spoon. Bake the shell in the lower third of the oven for 1 hour. Turn off the heat, leave the oven door ajar, and let the shell dry in the oven for at least 1 hour.

Make the filling:

   In the top of a double boiler set over hot water melt the chocolate, stirring until smooth, and let it cool to lukewarm. In a bowl with the mixer beat the egg whites with the salt until foamy, add the cream of tartar, and continue to beat the whites until they hold stiff peaks.

   In a large chilled bowl with the mixer beat the heavy cream with the dark rum until it holds stiff peaks. Fold the chocolate gently but thoroughly into the whipped cream and fold in the beaten egg whites.

   Spoon the chocolate filling into the meringue shell and chill the pie for at least 1 hour. Garnish with large dollops of the whipped cream.

CRANBERRY MERINGUE PIE

Yield:
one 9-inch pie

Equipment:
9-inch pie plate
hand-held electric
  mixer

In this recipe the meringue mixture is warmed over simmering water until the sugar is dissolved and then beaten until the egg whites hold stiff peaks. This method ensures a light, airy, successful meringue. One word of warning: Be sure to allow the cranberry filling to cool completely before spooning the meringue over it. If it is not cool, the meringue is likely to "weep," or separate, while being browned.

1 recipe pâte brisée *(page 116),
  rolled ⅛ inch thick, transferred to
  pie plate, and fitted in (see
  illustrations page 71)*

*raw rice or beans for weighting the
  shell*

FOR THE FILLING
*⅔ cup sugar
4 tablespoons cornstarch
1 tablespoon fresh lemon juice
3 egg yolks, beaten lightly
1½ cups water*

*1½ cups cranberries, picked over and
  rinsed
2 tablespoons unsalted butter, cut into
  pieces*

FOR THE MERINGUE
*4 egg whites at room temperature
⅓ cup sugar*

*¼ teaspoon cream of tartar
pinch of salt*

Trim the dough, leaving a ½-inch overhang. Crimp the edge of the shell decoratively (see illustrations page 72), prick the shell lightly with a fork, and chill it for 30 minutes, or freeze it for 15 minutes.

Preheat the oven to 425° F.

Line, weight, and blind-bake the shell (see illustrations page 115) in the lower third of the oven for 15 minutes. Remove the rice and foil carefully and bake the shell for 5 to 8 minutes more, or until golden. Let the shell cool in the pan on a rack.

Reduce the oven temperature to 350° F.

Make the filling: In a saucepan whisk together the sugar, cornstarch, lemon juice, egg yolks, and ½ cup of the water until the mixture is smooth. In another saucepan combine the cranberries and the remaining 1 cup water, bring the water to a boil, and simmer the mixture, covered, for 4 minutes. Purée the cranberry mixture in a blender and strain it through a fine sieve into a bowl, pressing hard on the solids. Stir the cranberry mixture into the yolk mixture, bring the mixture to a boil over moderate heat, whisking constantly, and cook it, whisking constantly, for 3 minutes. Remove the pan from the heat, add the butter, stirring until it is melted, and let the filling cool, stirring occasionally, for 15 minutes. Spread the filling in the shell and let it cool completely.

Make the meringue: In a metal bowl combine the egg whites, sugar, cream of tartar, and salt. Set the bowl over a pan of simmering water and stir the mixture until the sugar is dissolved. Remove the bowl from the pan and with the mixer beat the whites until they hold stiff, glossy peaks.

Spoon the meringue over the filling, smoothing it and covering the filling completely. Bake the pie in the middle of the oven for 8 to 10 minutes, or until the meringue is light golden. Let the pie cool in the pan on a rack and serve it at room temperature.

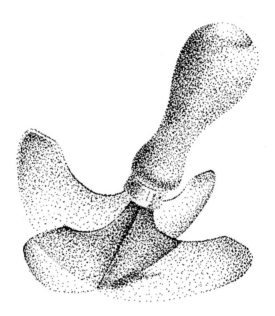

NUT PIES

What is it about nut pies that their fans love so? We think that it is the rather unlikely combination of a flaky pastry and a lustrous nut filling.

Pecan Pie (opposite), rich, sweet, and incredibly delicious, served warm with vanilla ice cream or whipped cream, is considered the ultimate pie by many. Peanut Butter Fudge Pie (page 96) is a type of candy pie especially popular with children. We've added espresso powder to the whipped cream accompaniment, however, for the adult in all of us. Note that these pies should be baked until puffed and just set. Like custard pies, the fillings will completely set while cooling, and, therefore, they must not be overbaked. They are both particularly good when served with whipped cream, which provides a welcome but toothsome relief from the sweetness of the fillings.

PECAN PIE

Yield:
one 11½-inch pie

Equipment:
11½-inch pie plate

1½ recipes pâte brisée (page 116), substituting 1 tablespoon sugar for the salt; rolled ⅛ inch thick, transferred to pie plate, and fitted in (see illustrations page 71)

raw rice or dried beans for weighting the shell

FOR THE FILLING
2 cups dark corn syrup
1 cup sugar
3 tablespoons unsalted butter, melted
3 tablespoons all-purpose flour

5 large eggs
1 tablespoon dark rum
½ teaspoon vanilla
2 cups pecan halves

sweetened whipped cream or vanilla ice cream as an accompaniment if desired

Trim excess dough from the sides of the shell, leaving a 1-inch overhang. Fold the overhang over the rim, pressing it onto the sides of the shell to form a decorative edge (see illustrations page 72). Prick the bottom of the shell with a fork and chill for 30 minutes.

Preheat the oven to 400° F.

Line, weight, and blind-bake the shell (see illustrations page 115) in the lower third of the oven for 15 minutes. Remove the rice and wax paper and bake the shell for 10 minutes more, or until lightly colored. Let the shell cool on a rack.

Reduce the oven temperature to 375° F.

Make the filling: In a large bowl combine the dark corn syrup, sugar, melted butter, and the flour. In a bowl lightly beat the eggs with the rum and the vanilla. Add the egg mixture to the sugar mixture and combine well. Arrange the pecans in the pastry shell and slowly pour in the filling.

Bake the pie in the middle of the oven for 40 minutes, or until it is puffed and set. Let the pie cool on a rack and serve it slightly warm with the whipped cream or ice cream.

PEANUT BUTTER FUDGE PIE

Yield:
9-inch pie

1 recipe pâte sucrée, *(page 117), rolled ⅛ inch thick, transferred to pie plate, and fitted in (see illustrations page 71)*

Equipment:
9-inch ceramic or glass pie plate

FOR THE FILLING

4 ounces unsweetened chocolate, chopped coarse
3 tablespoons unsalted butter
¼ cup smooth or chunky peanut butter
1 teaspoon vanilla
¾ cup plus 2 tablespoons granulated sugar

3 large eggs
1 cup dark corn syrup
½ cup milk
⅔ cup coarsely chopped roasted unsalted peanuts

1½ cups well-chilled heavy cream
1 tablespoon espresso powder

¼ cup confectioners' sugar

Trim off the excess dough, leaving a 1-inch overhang. Fold the overhang back over the edge, form a decorative ¼-inch rim above the plate (see illustrations page 72), and chill the shell for 30 minutes.

Preheat the oven to 325° F.

Make the filling: In the top of a double boiler set over simmering water melt the chocolate with the butter, stirring. In a large bowl beat the peanut butter, vanilla, granulated sugar, and the eggs and add the corn syrup and the milk in a stream, beating. Beat in the chocolate mixture and stir in the peanuts.

Pour the filling into the shell and bake the pie in the lower third of the oven for 55 minutes to 1 hour, or until the filling is just set. Let the pie cool on a rack and chill it for 2 hours, or until the filling is set. (The filling will set fully when the pie has cooled completely.)

In a well-chilled bowl beat the cream with the espresso powder and the confectioners' sugar until it holds soft peaks, transfer it to a serving bowl, and serve it with the pie.

Cassata (page 20)

Orange Génoise with Orange Buttercream (page 21)

Sugar Kirsch Torte (page 26)

Chocolate Mousse Cake with Ganache Icing (page 44)

Glazed Apple Cake (page 55)

Bûche de Noël (page 64)

Streusel Peach Pie (page 79)

Cranberry Maple Pear Pie (page 80), Pecan Pumpkin Pie (page 83)

Rhubarb Tart (page 120)

Apricot Frangipane Tart (page 127)

"American-style" cookies: Chocolate Chip Cookies (page 132),
Old-Fashioned Hermits with Lemon Glaze (page 136), Marbled Chocolate Butterscotch
Brownies (page 143), Chocolate Almond Macaroons (page 134)

Almond Tulipes with Strawberries and Whipped Cream (page 153)

Spice Cookie Hearts (page 158), Lemon Curd Tartlets (page 125)

Orange Poppy Seed Cake (page 48)

THE SIMPLE PLEASURES OF COFFEE

*A*ccording to legend, coffee was first discovered in Ethiopia by goatherds who noticed that their flocks stayed awake all night after munching on the leaves and berries of the coffee plant. Prized for its strong stimulative properties, coffee was used alternatively as a food, a wine, and a medicine before developing into a beverage approximately seven hundred years ago.

Today, coffee is valued for its distinctive flavor and aroma, its cultural appeal, and its singular ability to top off a fine meal or complement a delicate dessert. Coffee is the world's most popular beverage, and the average American consumes fourteen pounds worth of coffee beans annually. The finest beans are washed Arabicas, which produce the aromatic flavor and rich full body of the world's most expensive gourmet coffees.

Arabicas are slow growing, high-altitude mountain beans that thrive in semitropical climates. Their recognizably rich aroma and superior flavor are released during a deep roasting process, which gives the beans their characteristic color and texture. Expert coffee roasters take special care to protect the deep, full-bodied flavor and pure high-grown notes that are unique to the Arabica.

Although coffee has long been popular as a morning pick-me-up, it holds a much broader appeal in spectacular coffee-flavored mousses, ice creams, icings, and syrups. No longer a mere companion for the coffee-cake, coffee has now become a necessary element in any dessert menu.

Choosing a gourmet blend is the first step in brewing rich, non-bitter coffee. We recommend *Folgers Gourmet Supreme*, a blend of washed Arabicas that is conveniently available in the supermarket. Most blends use a vacuum seal to protect the integrity of the coffee, since fresh coffee beans begin to lose flavor almost immediately after roasting. By storing opened coffee in the refrigerator, you can extend shelf life from about five weeks to approximately one year.

When preparing to brew, choose distilled water, which contains none of the minerals in tap water that can interfere with or taint the coffee flavor. Never keep brewed coffee on a burner; instead, pour freshly brewed coffee directly into a thermos or other insulated container. Most importantly, clean your coffee maker thoroughly before brewing.

The real beauty of fine coffee is its simplicity. Subtle enough to serve with the most delicate pastries, hearty enough to stand up to the richest torte, coffee is inextricably tied to our urge to commune over a meal, to complement fine company with fine food. Whenever you plan dessert, plan to serve coffee.

TARTS

The difference between pies and tarts is really quite simple. A tart is basically free standing and usually open faced. The dough is formed in a tart pan or flan form with a removable rim so that upon being baked the shell can be removed from the pan. Because of this, a different type of pastry is required; one that is less fragile or flaky than pie dough. And the shell is usually prebaked, filled with fruit alone—fresh, dried, poached, stewed, or even puréed; fruit with cream or almond fillings or a layer of whipped cream; nuts combined with rich, sweet caramel; or even a simple jam filling made even more flavorful with cinnamon, nutmeg, and cloves if desired.

Tarts lend themselves to creative interpretation. Even if a round tart pan has been called for, there is no reason why the tart cannot be prepared in whichever form you prefer or why it cannot be formed into any shape you desire. This is the beauty of a tart as opposed to a pie. A pie takes the shape of the pie plate. A tart, because it is free standing, takes the shape you create. Experiment with tart or flan shapes that coordinate with the arrangement of the fruit. If a pie plate or cake pan is the only thing available, however, a tart shell can even be fashioned over the bottom of the inverted plate or pan and can be carefully removed after baking.

A good pastry cream is often an essential part of a good tart. It must be made well to result in a smooth, creamy, and flavorful cream. (Follow the instructions for making pastry cream on page 164.)

Even the most rural *pâtisserie* in France has an extraordinarily varied selection of tarts in its window. The French certainly know that the combination of healthful fruit or nut fillings and pastry is a nutritionally sound dessert and not too worrisome calorically. Tarts are certainly good for your spirit, and a better understanding and serious consideration of tarts as a homemade dessert would be a wonderful thing in our country and a welcome addition to our baking repertoires. Tarts are not difficult to prepare and for as easy as they really are, they are not made often enough.

TART DOUGHS

There are different types of tart doughs but there is one that has been used by *Gourmet* throughout the years and has always given superb results. This dough is called *pâte brisée* and is a combination of flour and butter or shortening that is blended until the mixture resembles coarse meal like the standard pie pastry (see illustrations page 73). However, at that point *pâte brisée* is lightly kneaded with the heel of the hand against a work surface in a process called *fraisage*, to distribute the fat evenly. This results in a crust of substance, one that is crisp but tender, strong enough to be free-standing yet not tough. Butter is the principal fat used in *pâte brisée* for its excellent flavor, but a portion of vegetable shortening is also incorporated for flakiness. You will notice in our "Pies" section, this same *pâte brisée* dough is called for as a pie crust. Although not required to stand alone, this crust is especially appropriate for certain types of pie fillings.

Another classic tart pastry is *pâte sucrée*, a richer, sweeter, more cookie-like dough that employs only butter and to which egg and sugar are added. The egg makes the dough less fragile and permits more handling without fear of overworking the dough.

In this chapter we have also included a recipe for Rich Whole-Wheat Pastry Dough, made, as its name indicates, with whole-wheat flour. This produces a wholesome, more substantially textured crust and its slightly nutty flavor perfectly complements the spicy apple and pecan filling in the recipe for Apple Pecan Whole-Wheat Tart.

After chilling the dough it may be rolled out as described in the Pie Dough introduction (page 71). (You can also simply pat the buttery dough into the tart pan.) As illustrated, the dough is rolled out and transferred to the tart pan by rolling it over and off the rolling pin, laying it loosely onto the pan. Using your fingertips or knuckles, carefully press the dough into the pan, being careful to press the dough against the fluted sides and into the fluted edges of the tart pan or flan ring. Fold back some of the excess dough to create a sufficiently thick edge around the tart. The easiest way to trim the tart dough is to roll the rolling pin across the edge of the tart pan, trimming it flush with the edge of the pan and cutting it neatly against the pan's sharp top edge, letting the excess dough fall off. The result will be a neatly lined pan with an attractive edge. (If desired, a decorative edge could be formed, as described in the introduction to pie doughs.) To line tartlet tins, arrange the tins so they touch one another, lay the dough over the tins, and roll the pin over the dough as shown, lining the individual tins as you go. Prick the shell or tins and chill.

The term "blind-baking" is often interpreted to mean prebaking a tart shell. While it does mean this, it also means something far more literal. The term refers to baking the shell or tins with the bottom surface covered so that it is not visible. The surface is lined first with wax paper, then completely covered with raw rice or dried beans, being sure to weight the indents of the scalloped bottom rim of the tart tin. The weight of the rice or beans will prevent the dough from shrinking or blistering while baking. The shell is then transferred to a baking sheet and is baked as directed. "Blind-baking" is an essential part of tart-making because it allows for fillings which would otherwise render the tart's bottom crust soggy and fillings which could not have been baked simultaneously with the bottom crust.

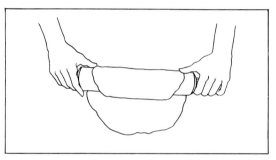

Rolling dough over rolling pin

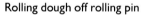

Rolling dough off rolling pin

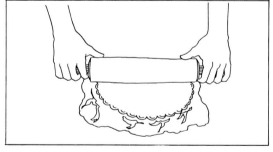

Trimming crust with pin

Pricking bottom of shell; weighting lined shell with raw rice; lined and weighted shell on baking sheet

PÂTE BRISÉE

Yield:
about 11 ounces
  dough
enough dough for one
  9- or 10-inch tart
  shell

Pâte brisée literally means "broken," or short, pastry in French. Short dough is light and has the discernible flavor of butter.

A specific technique, called *fraisage*, is used in making *pâte brisée*. By lightly smearing the dough across the work surface with the heel of the hand, the fat, in this case butter, is distributed throughout different layers of the pastry, thus rendering a tender yet firm crust. However, like all fine doughs, you do not want to overwork or overroll *pâte brisée*.

1¼ cups all-purpose flour
¾ stick (6 tablespoons) cold unsalted
  butter, cut into bits
2 tablespoons cold vegetable
  shortening

¼ teaspoon salt
3 tablespoons ice water

The dough may be frozen, wrapped in plastic and foil, for up to 1 month. To defrost, place in the refrigerator overnight.

In a large bowl with your fingertips or with two knives blend the flour, butter, vegetable shortening, and salt until the mixture resembles meal (see illustrations page 71). Add the ice water, toss the mixture until the water is incorporated, and form the dough into a ball. Knead the dough lightly with the heel of the hand against a smooth surface for a few seconds to distribute the fat evenly and re-form it into a ball. Dust the dough with flour and chill it, wrapped in wax paper, for at least 1 hour, or for up to 2 days.

Variation:

PÂTE BRISÉE: PROCESSOR METHOD: In a food processor fitted with the steel blade combine the flour, butter, vegetable shortening, and salt and process the mixture until it resembles coarse meal. Sprinkle the water over the mixture and process it until it comes together in large pieces about the size of pebbles. Transfer the dough to a work surface and if it is dry sprinkle it with 1 tablespoon more water. With the heel of your hand knead the dough against a smooth surface for a few seconds to distribute the fat evenly and form it into a ball. Dust the dough with flour and chill it, wrapped in wax paper, for at least 1 hour, or for up to 2 days.

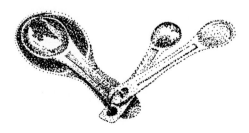

PÂTE SUCRÉE

Yield:
about 15 ounces
  dough
enough dough for one
  10-inch shell

Pâte sucrée means sweet pastry in French and describes crumbly sweetened pastry dough similar in texture and flavor to cookie dough. The dough produces remarkable results when made into free-standing tarts as this firmer cookie-like dough, due to the addition of egg, holds up better as a free-form tart shell. The dough also withstands more handling because the natural oils of the egg help prevent the development of the gluten due to flour and moisture. The *fraisage* method, described in the recipe for *pâte brisée* is also used in making *pâte sucrée*. Of course, in most instances *pâte brisée* and *pâte sucrée* are interchangeable, and this sweetened dough can be substituted for *pâte brisée* with simply sweeter results.

1½ cups all-purpose flour
¼ cup sugar
¼ teaspoon salt
1 stick plus 1 tablespoon (½ cup plus
  1 tablespoon) cold unsalted butter,
  cut into bits

1 large egg, beaten lightly
1 to 2 tablespoons ice water

The dough may be frozen, wrapped in plastic and foil, for up to 1 month. To defrost, place in the refrigerator overnight.

Variation:

In a large bowl with your fingertips or with two knives blend the flour, sugar, salt, and the butter until the mixture resembles meal (see illustrations page 71). Add the egg and 1 tablespoon of the water, toss the mixture until the liquid is incorporated, adding 1 more tablespoon of water if the mixture is dry, and form the dough into a ball. Knead the dough lightly with the heel of your hand against a smooth surface for a few seconds to distribute the fat evenly and re-form it into a ball. Dust the dough with flour and chill it, wrapped in wax paper, for 1 hour.

PÂTE SUCRÉE: PROCESSOR METHOD: In a food processor fitted with the plastic or steel blade combine the flour, sugar, salt, and butter and process the mixture until it resembles coarse meal. In a bowl combine the egg with 1 tablespoon of the water and sprinkle it over the flour mixture. Process the mixture until it comes together in large pieces about the size of pebbles and transfer the dough to a work surface. If the mixture is dry, sprinkle it with 1 more tablespoon water. With the heel of your hand knead the dough against a smooth surface for a few seconds to distribute the fat evenly and form it into a ball. Dust the dough with flour and chill it, wrapped in wax paper, for at least 1 hour, or for up to 2 days.

RICH WHOLE-WHEAT TART PASTRY

Yield:
about 12 ounces dough
enough dough for one 9- or 10-inch tart shell

½ cup all-purpose flour
½ cup whole-wheat flour
⅓ cup finely ground pecans
¾ stick (6 tablespoons) cold unsalted butter, cut into bits
2 tablespoons cold vegetable shortening, cut into bits
1½ teaspoons grated orange rind if desired

1 tablespoon sugar
½ teaspoon double-acting baking powder
⅛ teaspoon salt
3 to 4 tablespoons cold orange juice or ice water

The dough keeps chilled, covered, overnight. The dough keeps frozen, wrapped tightly in plastic wrap and aluminum foil, for up to 2 weeks. To defrost, place in the refrigerator overnight.

In a large bowl with your fingertips or with two knives blend the all-purpose flour, the whole-wheat flour, the pecans, butter, shortening, orange rind, if desired, sugar, baking powder, and the salt until the mixture resembles meal (see illustrations page 71). Add 3 tablespoons of the orange juice or ice water and toss the mixture until the liquid is incorporated, adding the additional tablespoon of liquid, or enough to form the dough into a ball. Knead the dough lightly with the heel of the hand against a smooth surface for a few seconds to distribute the fat evenly and re-form it into a ball. Dust the dough with flour and chill it, wrapped in wax paper, for 1 hour.

FRUIT TARTS

Fruit tarts are among the most impressive of desserts. While not difficult to execute, the combination of a buttery pastry or sugar cookie-like shell and ripe, juicy fruits with, perhaps, a liqueur-flavored pastry cream and a brilliant fruit glaze is too often reserved as a perfect dessert when dining out! In an attempt to bring the fruit tart back to its proper place, your dining table, we have included recipes for tarts with chocolate-glazed shells, dried fruits, and rhubarb. An especially appealing recipe is for Applesauce Tarts (page 121), using an applesauce made with green apples and with strips of vanilla-flavored hard sauce piped on top. Tartlets are simply small or individual tarts made in tartlet tins.

A simple tart of sliced apples is elevated to new heights with the addition of golden raisins, pecans, and orange liqueur, but retains its rustic nature by using a whole-wheat (albeit rich) crust.

PEAR AND CHOCOLATE TART

Yield:
one 9-inch tart

Equipment:
9-inch round tart pan
with removable rim
or a flan ring with a
baking sheet base
pastry brush

1 recipe pâte brisée *(page 116),
rolled ⅛ inch thick, transferred to
tart pan, and fitted in (see
illustrations page 115)*
*raw rice or dried beans for weighting
the shell*
2 cups water
1 cup sugar
*a 1-inch piece of vanilla bean or
1 teaspoon vanilla*

4 to 6 pears, peeled, halved, and cored
*6 ounces semisweet chocolate, chopped
coarse*
2 tablespoons unsalted butter
*½ cup apricot glaze (page 165) made
with 2 tablespoons Cognac, heated*
*⅔ cup sliced blanched almonds,
toasted lightly*
*whipped cream as an accompaniment
if desired*

Trim the edge of the dough with the rolling pin. Prick the shell with a fork and chill the shell for 30 minutes.

Preheat the oven to 400° F.

Line, weight, and blind-bake the shell (see illustrations page 115) on a baking sheet in the lower third of the oven for 15 minutes. Remove the rice and paper carefully.

Reduce the oven temperature to 375° F.

Bake the shell for 10 to 15 minutes more, or until golden. Let cool on a rack.

In a large heavy skillet combine the water and the sugar and cook the mixture until the sugar is dissolved. Add the vanilla bean and cook the syrup for 5 minutes. Add the pears and poach them for 15 to 25 minutes, depending on their degree of ripeness. Let the pears cool in the syrup and drain them on paper towels.

In the top of a double boiler set over hot water melt the chocolate, stirring until smooth, and stir in the butter. Brush the bottom of the shell with the chocolate and let set for 30 minutes. Arrange the poached pear halves in the shell decoratively, brush them well with the apricot glaze, and garnish the tart with the almonds. Serve with the whipped cream.

RHUBARB TART

Yield:
one 9¾-inch tart

Equipment:
9¾-inch tart pan with
  removable rim
pastry brush

The shell of this tart is initially baked for thirty minutes, then filled with stewed rhubarb as well as ¾ cup of syrup. Because of the weight of the filling and the syrup, the tart continues baking on a rack set on a baking sheet to facilitate its handling.

1 recipe pâte brisée *(page 116) substituting 2 teaspoons sugar for the salt; rolled ⅛-inch thick, transferred to tart pan, and fitted in (see illustrations page 115)*

raw rice or dried beans for weighting the shell

FOR THE STEWED RHUBARB
2⅓ cups sugar
1 cup water

about 3 pounds rhubarb, cut into 1¾-inch lengths (about 6 cups)

10 strawberries, hulled, with hulls reserved for garnish if desired

2 tablespoons brandy, or to taste

lightly whipped cream as an accompaniment if desired

Trim the edge of the dough with the rolling pin. Prick the shell with a fork and chill the shell for 30 minutes.

Preheat the oven to 400° F.

Line, weight, and blind-bake the shell (see illustrations page 115) in the lower third of the oven for 10 to 15 minutes, or until it begins to set. Carefully remove the rice and paper and bake the shell for 10 to 15 minutes more, or until lightly colored. Remove the shell from the pan, transfer it to a rack, and let it cool.

Make the stewed rhubarb:
In a skillet combine the sugar with the water and bring the mixture to a boil over moderately low heat, washing down any sugar crystals clinging to the sides of the pan with the brush dipped in cold water until the sugar is dissolved. Increase the heat to moderate and simmer the syrup for 5 minutes. Add half the rhubarb and simmer the mixture for 3 to 6 minutes, or until it is just soft, removing the pieces with a slotted spatula to a shallow dish. Simmer the remaining rhubarb in the syrup in the same manner, transferring it to the dish when it is just soft. Spoon the syrup over the rhubarb, let the mixture cool, and chill.

To assemble the tart:
Preheat the oven to 400° F.

As near to serving time as possible, with the shell still on the rack, transfer the rhubarb with a narrow metal slotted spatula to the shell, arranging the fruit in slightly overlapping rows. Reserve the syrup. Arrange the strawberries around the shell.

In a skillet reduce the reserved syrup over moderately high heat to ¾ cup and stir in the brandy. Spoon the warm syrup over the rhubarb and strawberries. Heat a baking sheet. Set the tart with the rack on the baking sheet and bake it in the middle of the oven for 10 minutes. Let the tart cool on the rack for 10 minutes and transfer it to a serving plate. If desired, replace the strawberry hulls for decoration. Serve the tart with the lightly whipped cream.

Photo on page 105.

APPLESAUCE TARTS

Yield:
twelve 2¾-inch tarts

Equipment:
twelve 2¾-inch tart tins
food mill
pastry brush
pastry bag fitted with small decorative tip

1 recipe pâte sucrée *(page 117)*
12 large unpeeled Granny Smith apples, quartered and cored
½ cup water
sugar to taste
cinnamon to taste
freshly ground pepper to taste
apricot jam, melted and cooled
1 recipe hard sauce (page 173)

Roll the dough ⅛ inch thick on a lightly floured surface. Cut the dough into 12 circles about an inch larger in diameter than the tart tins you are using. Ease the circles into the tart tins and pinch them into place. Or arrange the tart tins together, touching one another, to approximate the shape of the rolled-out dough. Drape the dough over the rolling pin and unroll it over the tins. Roll the rolling pin over the dough to cut it (see illustrations page 115). Prick the shells with a fork and chill them for about 30 minutes.

In a large saucepan combine the apples with the water and cook them, covered tightly, over moderate heat for about 20 minutes, or until soft. Force the apples through the food mill into a bowl and stir in the sugar, cinnamon, and pepper. (You should have about 3 cups applesauce.)

Preheat the oven to 400° F.

Bake the shells on a baking sheet in the lower third of the oven for about 8 to 10 minutes, or until golden. Let the shells cool on a rack. When the tins are cool enough to handle, remove the shells from the tins and allow them to cool on the rack.

Brush the bottoms and sides of the shells with the apricot jam and fill each shell with about ¼ cup of the applesauce. Fill the pastry bag with the hard sauce and pipe 4 thin strips of it in a lattice pattern over the applesauce in each tart.

DRIED APRICOT TART

Yield:
one 14- by 4½-inch
   tart

Equipment:
14- by 4½-inch tart
   pan with removable
   rim
pastry brush

The shell of this tart is prepared with *pâte sucrée* and is only partially blind baked. The tart is then filled and is baked for another half hour. The partial blind-baking can be done ahead of time if desired.

1 recipe pâte sucrée *(page 117)*
raw rice or dried beans for weighting
   the shell
1 pound dried apricots
½ cup sugar
¾ stick (6 tablespoons) cold unsalted
   butter, cut into bits

¾ cup apricot glaze (page 165),
   heated
6 halved blanched almonds (for
   procedure page 174)
lightly sweetened whipped cream as
   an accompaniment if desired

On a lightly floured surface roll the dough into a ⅛-inch-thick rectangle, at least 17 by 8 inches. Drape the dough over the rolling pin and unroll it over the tart pan. Fit the dough firmly into the pan and trim the edge of the dough with the rolling pin. Prick the bottom of the shell with a fork and chill the shell for 1 hour.

Preheat the oven to 400° F.

Line, weight, and blind-bake the shell (see illustrations page 115) in the lower third of the oven for 10 to 15 minutes, or until it begins to set. Carefully remove the rice and wax paper and bake the shell for 5 minutes more, or until it is lightly colored. Carefully remove the shell from the pan, transfer it with a large spatula to a rack, and let it cool.

Reduce the oven temperature to 375° F.

In a saucepan combine the apricots with enough water to cover them by ½ inch and bring the water to a boil over moderately high heat. Reduce the heat to low, simmer the apricots for 20 minutes, and let them cool in the water.

Transfer the shell to a baking sheet, drain the apricots, and arrange them, slightly overlapping, in crosswise rows in the shell. Sprinkle the apricots with the sugar, dot them with the butter, and bake the tart in the upper third of the oven for 30 minutes. (If the apricots have not become richly colored, put the tart under a preheated broiler for about 3 minutes.) Brush the hot tart with the apricot glaze, transfer it to a rack, and let it cool slightly. Decorate the center of the tart with the almonds, transfer the tart to a serving board, and serve it slightly warm with the whipped cream.

APPLE AND PECAN TART IN WHOLE-WHEAT CRUST

Yield:
one 9½-inch tart

Equipment:
9½-inch tart pan with
removable rim
pastry brush

*1 recipe rich whole-wheat tart pastry
(page 118), rolled ⅛-inch thick,
transferred to tart pan, and fitted in
(see illustrations page 115)*
⅓ cup golden raisins
1 tablespoon orange-flavored liqueur
*3 large McIntosh apples (about
1½ pounds), peeled, cored, and
sliced*
½ cup finely chopped pecans
*¾ stick (6 tablespoons) unsalted
butter, softened*

⅓ cup sugar
1 large egg, beaten lightly
1½ teaspoons grated orange rind
½ teaspoon vanilla
½ teaspoon cinnamon
⅛ teaspoon freshly grated nutmeg
*½ cup apricot glaze (page 165) made
with 1 tablespoon orange-flavored
liqueur, heated*

Trim the edge of the dough with the rolling pin. Prick the bottom of the shell with a fork and chill the shell for at least 30 minutes.

In a bowl toss the raisins with the liqueur and let them macerate for 30 minutes.

Preheat the oven to 375° F.

Arrange the apple slices, rounded side up (see illustration), in the tart pan and sprinkle them with the raisins, drained. In a bowl whisk together the pecans, butter, sugar, egg, orange rind, vanilla, cinnamon, and nutmeg until the mixture is combined. Spoon the filling over the apples, spreading it evenly. Bake the tart on a baking sheet in the lower third of the oven for 30 minutes. Transfer the tart to the middle of the oven and continue to bake it for 10 to 15 minutes longer, or until it is golden brown on top. Transfer to a rack.

While the tart is still warm spoon the glaze over the top. Let the tart cool on the rack. Serve the tart slightly warm or at room temperature.

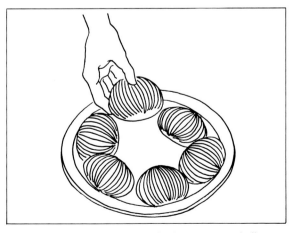

Arranging apple slices, rounded side up, in tart shell

PAPAYA TART WITH COCONUT PASTRY CREAM

Yield:
one 10-inch tart

Equipment:
10-inch tart pan with
  removable rim
hand-held electric
  mixer
pastry brush

1 recipe pâte sucrée (page 117), rolled ⅛-inch thick, transferred to tart pan, and fitted in (see illustrations page 115)

raw rice or dried beans for weighting the shell

FOR THE COCONUT PASTRY CREAM

1 cup milk
⅓ cup heavy cream
1 cup sweetened flaked coconut
3 egg yolks
⅓ cup sugar
2 tablespoons all-purpose flour

2 tablespoons cornstarch
2 tablespoons unsalted butter, cut into bits
1 tablespoon dark rum
½ teaspoon vanilla

½ cup apricot glaze (page 165) made with 1 tablespoon dark rum

1 papaya, peeled, halved, seeded, and cut into ⅛-inch-thick slices

Trim the edge of the dough with the rolling pin. Prick the shell with a fork and chill the shell for 30 minutes.

Preheat the oven to 400° F.

Line, weight, and blind-bake the shell (see illustrations page 115) on a baking sheet in the lower third of the oven for 15 minutes. Carefully remove the rice and paper. Reduce the oven temperature to 375° F. Bake the shell for 10 to 15 minutes more, or until golden. Let the shell cool on a rack.

Make the coconut pastry cream:

In a heavy saucepan bring the milk and cream to a simmer, stir in the coconut, and let the mixture stand for 15 minutes. In a large bowl with the mixer beat the yolks until combined, add the sugar, a little at a time, beating, and beat the mixture until light and lemon colored. Add the flour and the cornstarch, a little at a time, beating, and beat the mixture until smooth. Add the milk mixture, in a stream, beating, and beat the mixture

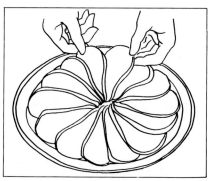

Arranging papaya slices decoratively in tart shell

until well combined. Transfer the mixture to the saucepan, bring it to a boil, whisking constantly, and simmer it over low heat for 3 minutes, or until it is thick and custard-like. Remove the pan from the heat, beat in the butter, rum, and vanilla and transfer the cream to a plate. Let the pastry cream cool, covered with a buttered round of wax paper, and chill it for at least 1 hour, or until cold.

Brush the bottom of the pastry shell with some of the apricot glaze and spoon the pastry cream into the shell, smoothing it into an even layer. Arrange the papaya slices decoratively over the cream (see illustration) and brush the papaya with the remaining glaze. Keep the tart chilled until ready to serve. The tart is best served within 1 to 1½ hours after assembly.

LEMON CURD TARTLETS

Yield:
ten 3-inch or fourteen to sixteen 2-inch tartlets

1 recipe pâte brisée *(page 116) made with an additional 1 tablespoon sugar; rolled ⅛ inch thick*

raw rice or dried beans for weighting the shell

Equipment:
4-inch or 3-inch round fluted cutter
ten 3-inch or fourteen to sixteen 2-inch tartlet tins
hand-held electric mixer

FOR THE LEMON CURD FILLING
4 egg yolks
½ cup sugar
½ stick (¼ cup) unsalted butter

½ cup well-chilled heavy cream

juice of 2 lemons, strained
1 teaspoon grated lemon rind

16 blanched almonds (for procedure page 174), toasted lightly

With the fluted cutter cut out rounds from the dough 1 inch larger than the tins. Press the rounds firmly into the tins, prick them with a fork, and chill them for 1 hour.

Preheat the oven to 400° F.

Line, weight, and blind-bake the shells (see illustrations page 115) on a baking sheet in the middle of the oven for 10 minutes. Carefully remove the rice and paper and bake the shells for 5 to 8 minutes more, or until lightly colored. Remove the shells from the tins and let them cool on a rack.

Make the lemon curd filling:

In a heavy saucepan combine the egg yolks, sugar, butter, and the lemon juice. Cook the mixture over medium low heat, stirring, until the butter is melted and the custard is thick enough to coat a spoon. Do not let it boil. Transfer the custard to a bowl and stir in the lemon rind. Let the custard cool, cover it with a round of buttered wax paper, and chill it.

In a chilled bowl with the mixer beat the heavy cream until it forms soft peaks. Fold one fourth of the cream into the lemon curd, combine it well, and fold in the remaining cream. Just before serving, divide the filling among the shells and top each tartlet with a blanched almond.

Photo on page 108.

Variation:

PINK GRAPEFRUIT CURD TARTLETS: In a small saucepan boil ½ cup strained fresh pink grapefruit juice until it is reduced to about 2 tablespoons, add 2½ tablespoons sugar and ½ stick (¼ cup) unsalted butter, cut into bits, and simmer the mixture, stirring, until the sugar is dissolved. In a small bowl beat 1 large egg, add the hot liquid in a slow stream, whisking, and return the mixture to the pan. Cook the mixture over moderately low heat, stirring, until it is thickened to the consistency of hollandaise, but do not let it boil. Transfer the curd to a bowl and let it cool, covered with a lightly buttered round of wax paper.

FRANGIPANE-FILLED AND NUT TARTS

Frangipane refers to an almond-flavored creamy filling combining eggs, sugar, butter, and ground almonds. When baked, the frangipane becomes almost cake-like in texture. Frangipane can be used as a separate layer in a tart, baked and then filled or the frangipane and filling can be baked together; as the frangipane bakes, it puffs up and sets around the fruit. In our recipe for Apricot Frangipane Tart (page 127), the almond cream is spread in the shell and topped with the fruit. After baking, the apricot halves are encircled by golden puffs of the frangipane, resulting in a rustic, pebbly appearance.

Pecan Caramel Tart (page 128) and Macadamia Nut Tartlets (page 129) are buttery, sweet, and luscious. Because of the richness of nut tarts, they are best served in small portions or as tartlets.

APRICOT FRANGIPANE TART

Yield:
one tart, 11¼ by 8 by 1 inches

Equipment:
rectangular tart pan with removable fluted rim, 11¼ by 8 by 1 inches
baking sheet
hand-held electric mixer
pastry brush

Frangipane is an almond cream filling or a rich vanilla custard finished with crushed macaroons. When baked, frangipane takes on a cake-like texture.

1½ recipes pâte brisée (page 116), rolled ⅛-inch thick, transferred to tart pan, and fitted in (see illustrations page 115)
1 stick (½ cup) unsalted butter, cut into bits and softened
⅓ cup plus 2 teaspoons sugar
2 large eggs
1 cup blanched almonds (for procedure page 174), ground
1 teaspoon vanilla
a 2-pound can apricot halves, drained
½ cup apricot glaze (page 165)

Trim the edge of the dough with the rolling pin. Prick the shell with a fork and chill the shell for 30 minutes.

Preheat the oven to 350° F. and preheat the baking sheet.

In a bowl with the mixer cream the butter, add ⅓ cup of the sugar, and beat the mixture until fluffy. Add the eggs, one at a time, beating well after each addition, and beat in the almonds and the vanilla. Spread the frangipane mixture in the shell, top it with the apricot halves cut sides up, and bake the tart on the baking sheet in the lower third of the oven for 40 minutes, or until the filling is golden and set.

Preheat the broiler.

Sprinkle the tart with the remaining 2 teaspoons sugar and put it under the broiler about 6 inches from the heat for 2 to 3 minutes, or until the filling is browned. Brush the tart with the apricot glaze, let it cool, and remove the rim of the pan.

Photo on page 105.

PECAN CARAMEL TART

Yield:
one 10-inch tart

Equipment:
10-inch decorative
   flan form, 1 inch
   deep
baking sheet
candy thermometer

This tart with its deliciously sweet filling that is cooked, not baked, is surprisingly confection-like in nature and should be served in thin wedges.

1 recipe pâte brisée *(page 116), rolled ⅛ inch thick, transferred to flan form set on the baking sheet, and fitted in (see illustrations page 115)*
raw rice or dried beans for weighting the shell
1 stick (½ cup) unsalted butter, cut into pieces

2 cups firmly packed light brown sugar
⅓ cup dark corn syrup
4 cups pecan halves
½ cup heavy cream
¼ teaspoon ground allspice
2 tablespoons dark rum

Trim the edge of the dough with the rolling pin. Prick the bottom of the shell with a fork and chill the shell for 30 minutes.

Preheat the oven to 425° F.

Line, weight, and blind-bake the shell (see illustrations page 115) in the lower third of the oven for 10 minutes. Remove the rice and paper carefully, bake the shell for 5 to 10 minutes more, or until it is golden, and let it cool on the baking sheet. Remove the shell from the flan form and arrange it on a serving plate.

In a heavy saucepan melt the butter, add the sugar and corn syrup, and cook the mixture over moderately low heat, stirring, with a wooden spoon, for 7 to 10 minutes, or until the candy thermometer registers 260° F. Remove the pan from the heat, add the pecan halves, heavy cream, and allspice, and stir the mixture until combined well. Cook the mixture over low heat, stirring, for 5 minutes, or until the candy thermometer registers 200° F. Let the mixture cool for 5 minutes, stir in the rum, and spoon the mixture into the shell. Let the tart cool completely and chill it for at least 2 hours or overnight.

When it is cold, cut the tart into thin wedges or bite-size pieces with a knife dipped in hot water and let it stand at room temperature for 30 minutes.

MACADAMIA NUT TARTLETS

Yield:
6 tartlets

Equipment:
six 4-inch tartlet tins
5-inch round cutter
pastry brush

½ recipe pâte brisée *(page 116)*
⅔ cup sugar
3 tablespoons water
½ cup heavy cream, heated

1 cup whole macadamia nuts, chopped coarse and toasted
3 tablespoons unsalted butter, cut into tablespoons

Follow the directions for forming and baking tartlet shells as directed for Lemon Curd Tartlets (page 125).

In a heavy saucepan combine the sugar with the water and cook the mixture over moderate heat, washing down any sugar crystals clinging to the sides of the pan with the brush dipped in cold water until golden. Add the cream, a little at a time, and stir the mixture until smooth. Stir in the nuts and add the butter, one tablespoon at a time. Cook the mixture, stirring, for 3 minutes and let it cool for 5 minutes. Spoon the filling into the shells. Let the tartlets cool to room temperature before serving.

COOKIES

*W*e don't think about it every day, but in truth there is a glorious variety to the *kinds* of cookie that can be made. And it is this very variety that explains the cookie's universal appeal. There is a cookie for everyone.

We begin with that great beginner's cookie—the drop—for some of us the first recipe we ever made and the one that started us on an irrevocable infatuation with all things baked. Imagine what life would be like without the chocolate chip cookie. Moreover, imagine what it would be like without the quest for the *perfect* chocolate chip cookie. Growing up without hermits or macaroons? Couldn't have been done.

Along these simple lines is the next type—the icebox, or refrigerator, cookie. You could describe it as a good friend, thin but reliable. Better yet, thanks to technology, icebox cookies can now be ever at the ready.

The basic cookie becomes more complex with the bar variety, an inspired combination of some sweet crust topped with a preserve, or toffee crunch, or a lemony curd. While bar cookies may never be confused with pastry, they can be employed to cast a similar spell. They are for many the hands-down all-out favorite, bar none.

Then there is a group of cookies that we are choosing to call molded—specifically shaped—which include ladyfingers and those French creations, *tulipes*.

Lastly, there are rolled cookies. They will require the same touch that is needed for dough-making in general. Cool hands, if you will.

DROP COOKIES

We have called the drop cookie that great beginner's cookie, and it is just that. Drop cookies are simple, and no less good for it, satisfying, and easy to make. It is usually a one-bowl batter, requiring no elaborate kitchen equipment, using ingredients that most of us have on hand at any given moment, including a goodly assortment of various kinds of chocolate chips.

Three caveats apply when it comes to making drop cookies:

- The batters, which sometimes can be stiff, must be thoroughly combined.

- When dropping the batter by the spoonful onto the baking sheet, be sure to leave a sufficient amount of space between the mounds. Drop cookies spread during baking and too many's the time we have ended up with one giant cookie instead of the three dozen that were called for.

- If you are making a recipe for the first time, cool the baked cookies as suggested. After that you can adjust cooling times to achieve the texture you most prefer. Cookies tend to crisp as they cool.

Which leads us to that most pleasurable thought: Drop cookies can never be made just once. They must be tasted, tested and experimented with, remade, and perfected. They are best made on the spur of the moment. Their variety can be endlessly pleasing.

CHOCOLATE CHIP COOKIES

Yield:
about 55 cookies

Equipment:
hand-held electric mixer

Everyone's idea of the "perfect" chocolate chip cookie is different. These have a delicious brown sugar flavor, and their texture will please both the chewy and crispy fans.

2 cups all-purpose flour
½ teaspoon salt
½ teaspoon baking soda
¼ teaspoon cinnamon
2 sticks (1 cup) unsalted butter, softened

¾ cup firmly packed dark brown sugar
¾ cup granulated sugar
1 large egg
1 teaspoon vanilla
1 package (12 ounces) semisweet chocolate morsels

Preheat the oven to 375° F.

In a bowl combine the flour, salt, baking soda, and the cinnamon.

In another bowl with the mixer cream the butter well. Gradually add the sugars, mixing well after each addition, and cream until light and fluffy. Add the egg and the vanilla and beat well.

Add the dry ingredients gradually to the butter mixture, combining well after each addition. Stir in the chocolate morsels.

Drop the dough by teaspoonfuls 2 inches apart onto ungreased baking sheets. (For a crisper cookie, flatten the cookie slightly with the back of a wet spoon.) Bake in the middle of the oven for 10 to 12 minutes. Transfer the cookies with a spatula to a rack and let cool. The cookies will become crisper as they cool. If you prefer the cookies softer, do not cool them on a rack.

Photo on page 106.

Variations: PECAN CHOCOLATE CHIP COOKIES: Add 1 cup pecans, chopped and lightly toasted, to the cookie batter and bake as directed.

RAISIN CHOCOLATE CHIP COOKIES: Add 1 cup raisins to the cookie batter and bake as directed.

CHOCOLATE CHUNK COOKIES

Yield:
about 48 cookies

Equipment:
hand-held electric mixer

2 sticks (1 cup) unsalted butter, softened
1 cup firmly packed light brown sugar
½ cup granulated sugar
1 teaspoon vanilla
2 large eggs

2 ounces semisweet chocolate, melted and cooled, plus an additional 10 ounces semisweet chocolate, chopped coarse into ½-inch chunks
2 cups all-purpose flour
1 teaspoon salt
1 teaspoon baking soda

In a large bowl with the mixer cream the butter, add the brown sugar and granulated sugar, a little at a time, beating, and beat until fluffy. Stir in the vanilla and add the eggs, one at a time, beating well after each addition. Stir in the melted chocolate.

Into a bowl sift together the flour, salt, and baking soda. Beat the flour mixture into the batter in 3 batches, combining the mixture well, and stir in the coarsely chopped chocolate. Chill the dough, wrapped in plastic wrap, for 30 minutes, or until just firm.

Preheat the oven to 375° F.

Put rounded teaspoons of the dough 3 inches apart on ungreased baking sheets. Bake the cookies in the middle of the oven for 8 minutes, or until the edges are golden, and transfer them with a spatula to racks to cool.

Store in airtight containers with a slice of bread (to keep the cookies moist and chewy) for several days.

Variations: RAISIN CHOCOLATE CHUNK COOKIES: Plump 1 cup raisins in boiling water to cover for 45 minutes and drain well. Reduce the amount of coarsely chopped chocolate to 8 ounces. Stir in raisins when adding the chopped chocolate.

WALNUT CHOCOLATE CHUNK COOKIES: Reduce the amount of coarsely chopped chocolate to 8 ounces and stir in 1 cup chopped walnuts with the chopped chocolate.

ALMOND MACAROONS

Yield:
about 36 macaroons

Equipment:
parchment paper
food processor fitted
with steel blade

Store in layers
separated by wax
paper in airtight
containers.

A chewy macaroon, rich in almond flavor.

*1 cup whole blanched almonds (for
procedure page 174)*
1 cup sugar

¼ teaspoon almond extract
2 egg whites at room temperature

Line baking sheets with the parchment paper and preheat the oven to 300° F.

In the food processor or in a blender grind the almonds with the sugar to a powder. Transfer the mixture to a bowl and blend in the almond extract and the egg whites, one at a time, until the mixture is combined well. Drop the batter by teaspoons 2 inches apart onto the baking sheets and bake in the middle of the oven for 20 to 25 minutes, or until lightly golden. Let the macaroons cool and peel them off the paper.

COCONUT MACAROONS

Yield:
about 18 macaroons

Equipment:
hand-held electric
mixer

Store in layers
separated by wax
paper in an airtight
container.

3 egg whites at room temperature
1¼ cups sifted confectioners' sugar
1 teaspoon vanilla

*2 cups flaked sweetened coconut or
2 cups grated fresh coconut
(for procedure page 174)*
¼ cup sifted all-purpose flour

Butter and flour a baking sheet and preheat the oven to 325° F.

In a bowl with the mixer beat the egg whites until frothy. Gradually beat in the confectioners' sugar and the vanilla and continue to beat the whites until very stiff. Combine the coconut with the flour and fold the mixture into the egg whites. Drop the batter by tablespoons 2 inches apart onto the baking sheet and bake in the middle of the oven for 20 minutes, or until lightly golden and slightly firm to the touch. Transfer immediately to racks and let cool completely.

CHOCOLATE ALMOND MACAROONS

Yield:
about 20 macaroons

*3 ounces unsweetened chocolate,
chopped coarse*
*1 cup whole blanched almonds (for
procedure page 174)*
1 cup sugar

½ teaspoon almond extract
2 egg whites
*20 slivered blanched almonds for
garnish*

Equipment:
parchment paper
food processor fitted
  with steel blade
pastry bag fitted with
  large star tip

Store in layers
separated by wax
paper in airtight
containers.

Line a baking sheet with the parchment paper and preheat the oven to 300° F.

In a small saucepan melt the chocolate over low heat, stirring until the mixture is smooth, and let cool.

In the food processor or in a blender grind the almonds with the sugar to a powder. Transfer the mixture to a bowl and blend in the almond extract and the egg whites, one at a time, until the mixture is well combined. Add the melted chocolate and combine well. Using the pastry bag pipe out the batter in 1-inch diameter rosettes 2 inches apart onto the prepared baking sheet. (Or drop the batter by tablespoons 2 inches apart onto the sheet.) Garnish each macaroon with a slivered almond and bake in the middle of the oven for 20 to 25 minutes, or until the cookies are firm to the touch. Let the macaroons cool and peel them off the paper.

Photo on page 106.

APPLESAUCE BRAN COOKIES

Yield:
about 48 cookies

Equipment:
hand-held electric
  mixer

Here is the classic soft and cakey applesauce spice cookie, with the healthful addition of bran.

¾ cup sifted all-purpose flour
¾ cup sifted whole-wheat flour
¾ cup bran flakes cereal
½ teaspoon baking soda
¼ teaspoon salt
1½ teaspoons cinnamon
¾ teaspoon ground ginger
¾ teaspoon freshly grated nutmeg
½ teaspoon ground cloves
1 stick (½ cup) unsalted butter,
  softened

½ cup solid vegetable shortening,
  softened
1 cup sugar
1 teaspoon vanilla
1 large egg
1 cup applesauce
1 cup raisins
¾ cup chopped walnuts, toasted
  lightly

Preheat the oven to 350° F.

In a bowl combine the all-purpose flour, whole-wheat flour, bran flakes, baking soda, salt, cinnamon, ginger, nutmeg, and the cloves.

In a large bowl with the mixer cream the butter and shortening well. Add the sugar, a little at a time, and cream the mixture until light and fluffy. Add the vanilla and the egg and combine well. Gradually add the dry ingredients alternately with the applesauce, beating well after each addition. Stir in the raisins and the walnuts. (The dough will be soft.)

Drop the dough by heaping teaspoonfuls about 2 inches apart onto ungreased baking sheets and bake in the middle of the oven for 8 to 10 minutes, or until lightly golden. Let the cookies cool on the baking sheets for 1 minute, transfer them with a spatula to racks, and let cool completely.

OLD-FASHIONED HERMITS WITH LEMON GLAZE

Yield:
about 48 cookies

Equipment:
hand-held electric
  mixer

A splendid interpretation of an American classic, these hermits are iced with lemon glaze. If time is short, however, they are equally delicious unglazed or sprinkled with confectioners' sugar.

1¾ cups sifted all-purpose flour
½ teaspoon baking soda
½ teaspoon salt
½ teaspoon cinnamon
½ teaspoon freshly grated nutmeg
½ teaspoon ground ginger
½ teaspoon ground cloves
½ cup solid vegetable shortening,
  softened

½ stick (¼ cup) unsalted butter,
  softened
1 cup firmly packed dark brown sugar
1 large egg
½ teaspoon vanilla
2 tablespoons water
1 cup raisins
1 cup coarsely chopped walnuts,
  lightly toasted

FOR THE LEMON GLAZE
1 cup sifted confectioners' sugar

2 tablespoons fresh lemon juice

Butter baking sheets and preheat the oven to 350° F.

In a bowl combine the flour, baking soda, salt, cinnamon, nutmeg, ginger, and the cloves and reserve.

In another bowl with the mixer cream together the shortening and the butter. Add the brown sugar and cream the mixture until light and fluffy. Add the egg, vanilla, and the water and beat well. Gradually add the dry ingredients to the mixture, mixing well after each addition, and beat until smooth. Stir in the raisins and the walnuts and combine well.

Drop the dough by teaspoonfuls 2 inches apart onto the baking sheets. Flatten the cookies slightly with the back of a spoon dipped in cold water and bake them in the middle of the oven for 15 minutes. With a metal spatula transfer the cookies to racks to cool slightly.

Make the lemon glaze:

Combine the confectioners' sugar and the lemon juice and mix well.

While the cookies are still warm, spread about ½ teaspoon glaze on each cookie or simply dip the top surface of the cookie into the glaze. Let cool on the racks.

Photo on page 106.

OATMEAL RAISIN COOKIES

Yield:
48 cookies

Equipment:
hand-held electric mixer

1½ sticks (¾ cup) unsalted butter, softened
1 cup firmly packed dark brown sugar
¼ cup granulated sugar
2 large eggs
1 teaspoon vanilla
1 cup all-purpose flour
½ teaspoon baking soda
½ teaspoon cinnamon
¼ teaspoon salt
¼ teaspoon freshly grated nutmeg
2½ cups quick-cooking oats
1 cup raisins

Butter baking sheets and preheat the oven to 350° F.

In a bowl with the mixer cream the butter until fluffy. Add the dark brown sugar and granulated sugar and continue creaming until smooth. Add the eggs and the vanilla and blend well.

Combine the flour, baking soda, cinnamon, salt, and the nutmeg. Add the dry ingredients to the sugar mixture and blend well. Stir in the oats and the raisins and combine well.

Drop the dough by teaspoonfuls 2 inches apart onto the baking sheets. Flatten the cookies slightly with the back of a spoon dipped in cold water and bake them in the middle of the oven for 12 to 15 minutes, or until golden and slightly firm to the touch. With a metal spatula transfer the cookies immediately to a wire rack to cool.

Variation:

OATMEAL WALNUT COOKIES: Substitute 1 cup walnuts, toasted lightly and chopped coarse, for the raisins.

ICEBOX COOKIES

Icebox cookies, also known as refrigerator cookies, are singularly satisfying. Once the dough is made—and it is a very easy dough to combine and shape into a log—cookies can simply be sliced off the log and the log returned to the refrigerator. Or frozen, the dough will keep up to three months. The cookies can even be sliced extremely thin when the dough is still frozen for very crisp cookies. In short, cookies await, on demand, pending the mere preheating of the oven.

Icebox cookies are thin-cut and crispy when baked. Some are enhanced with butterscotch and orange and smell perfectly wonderful when baking. They are good accompaniments to fruit desserts, ice creams or sorbets, and some not-too-sweet puddings. You also might consider a tin of them and a festive package of the dough as a unique present during the holidays. There is very little to worry about, but lots to enjoy, when it comes to icebox cookies.

ORANGE MELTAWAYS

Yield:
about 40 cookies

Equipment:
hand-held electric
  mixer

It is the combination of confectioners' sugar and cornstarch in this recipe that renders an extremely tender "meltaway" cookie.

1½ sticks (¾ cup) unsalted butter,
  softened
½ cup sifted confectioners' sugar
1 cup sifted all-purpose flour

½ cup cornstarch
4 teaspoons grated orange rind
1 teaspoon vanilla
¼ cup granulated sugar

In a large bowl with the mixer cream together the butter and confectioners' sugar until light and fluffy. Into a bowl sift together the flour and cornstarch and stir the mixture into the butter mixture. Stir in the orange rind and vanilla and chill the dough, covered, for 1 hour, or until firm enough to shape.

Form the dough into a 10-inch log on a doubled sheet of wax paper. Using the wax paper as a guide, roll the dough tightly into a smooth 10-inch roll. Chill, wrapped in the wax paper and aluminum foil, in the freezing compartment of the refrigerator for at least 2 hours. (At this point the dough may be frozen.)

Butter baking sheets lightly and preheat the oven to 375° F.

Onto a sheet of wax paper sprinkle the granulated sugar and in it roll the dough. Cut the dough into ¼-inch slices with a sharp knife. Arrange the slices 2 inches apart on the baking sheets and bake them in the middle of the oven for 10 minutes, or until the edges are golden. Transfer the cookies to racks to cool.

BUTTERSCOTCH COOKIES

Yield:
48 cookies

Equipment:
hand-held electric
  mixer

1¾ cups sifted all-purpose flour
½ teaspoon baking soda
¼ teaspoon salt
1 stick (½ cup) unsalted butter,
  softened

1¼ cups firmly packed light brown
  sugar
1 large egg
1 teaspoon vanilla

Into a bowl sift together the flour, baking soda, and the salt. In another bowl with the mixer cream together the butter and the sugar until fluffy. Add the egg and vanilla and beat until smooth. Add the flour mixture gradually, beating well after each addition, and blend the dough well.

On a piece of wax paper form the dough into a log 1½ inches in diameter, using the paper as a guide. Chill the log, wrapped in the wax paper and foil, in the freezing compartment of the refrigerator for 2 hours. (At this point the dough may be frozen.)

Preheat the oven to 375° F.

Cut the log into ⅛-inch slices with a sharp knife and arrange the cookies 2 inches apart on ungreased baking sheets. Bake in the middle of the oven for 10 to 12 minutes, or until the edges are golden. (Do not underbake the cookies.) Transfer the cookies with a metal spatula to racks to cool. The cookies will become very crisp as they cool.

Variation: **BUTTERSCOTCH PECAN ICEBOX COOKIES:** Add ¾ cup finely chopped pecans to the dough and bake as above.

BAR COOKIES

For many this variety of cookie is the *sine qua non* of sweets. Imagine combining a buttery dough, sometimes studded with nuts, sometimes not, with a topping like chocolate pecan toffee or brown-sugar-sweetened cranberries. The cookie bakes and you have two splendid layers—the best of all possible worlds—tender pastry covered with the combination of choice, be it raspberry jam (as in our splendid Linzer bars) or tart lemon curd. Easier than pie, baked in one pan, bar cookies are cut into pieces and are also sometimes known as squares.

In this category we are also including that all-time favorite: the brownie. We have the classic fudge brownie, made with unsweetened chocolate, butter, flour, eggs, and walnuts. This is what some of us remember as our first brownie; the simplest and the best. Then we have buttery fudge brownies, made with not only two kinds of chocolate but also twice the amount of butter, a dash of bourbon, and some pecans. Nontraditionalist are these and not for the faint of heart. We've also included a recipe for cream cheese brownies in which the chocolate batter is enlivened with cinnamony whipped cream cheese. These, too, are rich and luxurious and curiously savory. An assortment of brownies would not be complete without a recipe for blondies, non-chocolate brownies with lots of brown sugar, chocolate chips, and chopped nuts. And because there can never be enough brownie recipes we have appended one last—marbled chocolate butterscotch brownies—which encompasses just about everything, including whole-wheat flour, and not just for salutary effect.

In making bar cookies—and it is a pure pleasure to do so—there are several items to remember:

■ Should the bar have a pastry base, the less the dough is handled, the flakier it will be. Also, in lining the pan, remember to pat the dough in; do not force it. In our recipes there is usually enough butter involved to meld the base as it bakes. The dough should be evenly spread, but it does not have to be a perfectly conformed layer.

■ Lastly, let bar cookies cool as directed in the recipes. They can be difficult to cut if not allowed to come to the proper temperature.

A postscript: It is our experience that bar cookies do not store well, and some, like Lemon Squares (page 146), should not be refrigerated at all. We consider that all to the good. Once made, they should be eaten, and remade.

As to the whole issue of brownies—how long do they cook, do you like them chewy or cake-like, are they better frozen or just barely thawed—we leave all of those refinements to you. We have provided the takeoff points. As far as brownies and bar cookies go—and these tend to be highly personalized matters—we leave the destination of these grand recipes up to you.

CLASSIC FUDGE BROWNIES

Yield:
16 brownies

Equipment:
8-inch square baking
  pan
hand-held electric
  mixer

A traditional recipe for the American favorite.

3 ounces unsweetened chocolate,
  chopped coarse
1 stick (½ cup) unsalted butter, cut
  into bits
¾ cup sifted all-purpose flour
½ teaspoon double-acting baking
  powder

pinch of salt
2 large eggs
1¼ cups sugar
1 teaspoon vanilla
1 cup chopped walnuts

Butter and flour the baking pan and preheat the oven to 350° F.

In a small heavy saucepan melt the chocolate and butter over low heat, stirring until the mixture is smooth, and let the mixture cool completely. Into a bowl sift together the flour, baking powder, and salt. In a large bowl with the mixer beat the eggs, add the sugar, a little at a time, beating, and beat the mixture at high speed for 3 minutes, or until thick and pale. Stir in the chocolate mixture and the vanilla, add the flour mixture, stirring until the mixture is blended well, and stir in the walnuts. Pour the batter into the baking pan, smoothing the top, and bake it in the middle of the oven for 25 to 30 minutes, or until it pulls away slightly from the sides of the pan and a cake tester inserted in the center comes out with crumbs adhering to it. Let the brownies cool completely in the pan before cutting them into squares.

Variation:

CLASSIC FUDGE BROWNIES WITH CHOCOLATE FUDGE ICING: Have ready chocolate fudge icing (page 172). Let brownies cool as above, spread them with frosting, and let the frosting set for 30 minutes.

CREAM CHEESE BROWNIES

Yield:
16 brownies

Equipment:
9-inch square baking pan
hand-held electric mixer

FOR THE CREAM CHEESE FILLING

5 ounces cream cheese at room temperature
2 tablespoons unsalted butter, softened
¼ cup sugar

1 large egg
½ teaspoon vanilla
¼ teaspoon cinnamon

FOR THE CHOCOLATE BATTER

4 ounces semisweet chocolate, chopped coarse
3 tablespoons unsalted butter, cut into bits
½ cup sifted all-purpose flour
½ teaspoon double-acting baking powder

¼ teaspoon salt
2 large eggs
¾ cup sugar
1 teaspoon vanilla
½ cup toasted and ground walnuts

Butter the baking pan and preheat the oven to 350° F.

Make the cream cheese filling:

In a bowl with the mixer cream the cream cheese with the butter until smooth. Gradually add the sugar, creaming until fluffy. Add the egg, vanilla, and cinnamon and beat the mixture well.

Make the chocolate batter:

In a saucepan melt the chocolate with the butter over very low heat. Cool and reserve. Combine the flour, baking powder, and salt.

In a bowl with the mixer beat the eggs until foamy. Gradually add the sugar, beating at high speed for 3 to 4 minutes, until pale yellow and thickened. Stir the flour mixture into the egg mixture, beating well. Blend in the reserved melted chocolate and stir in the vanilla and ground walnuts.

Spread half the chocolate batter evenly in the bottom of the baking pan. Spread the cheese mixture over the chocolate mixture. Drop the remaining chocolate batter in dollops over the cheese mixture. With a knife then swirl through the top two layers, creating a marbelized effect. Try not to disturb the bottom chocolate layer. Bake in the middle of the oven for 35 to 40 minutes, or until a cake tester inserted in the center comes out barely moist, with crumbs adhering to it. Let cool in the pan on a rack for at least 3 to 4 hours. Cut into sixteen 2¼-inch squares.

These brownies should be stored in the refrigerator and should not be frozen.

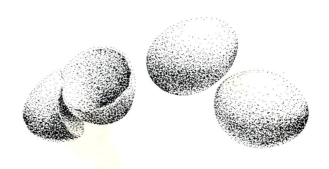

BUTTERY FUDGE BROWNIES

Yield:
30 brownies

Equipment:
baking pan, 13 by 9 by
  2 inches
hand-held electric
  mixer

This fudge brownie is twice as buttery and rich as our classic and contains both bourbon and pecans for a Southern touch.

2 ounces unsweetened chocolate,
  chopped coarse
2 ounces semisweet chocolate, chopped
  coarse
2 sticks (1 cup) unsalted butter,
  softened
1½ cups sugar

3 large eggs
1 teaspoon vanilla
1 cup sifted all-purpose flour
pinch of salt
1 cup chopped pecans
1½ tablespoons bourbon

Butter and flour the baking pan and preheat the oven to 350° F.

   In a small heavy saucepan melt both chocolates with 1 stick of the butter, cut into pieces, over low heat, stirring until smooth, and let cool completely. In a large bowl with the mixer cream together the remaining 1 stick butter and the sugar and beat until light and fluffy. Add the eggs, one at a time, beating well after each addition, and stir in the vanilla and the chocolate mixture. Add the flour and the salt, stirring until the mixture is blended well, and stir in the pecans and bourbon. Pour the batter into the baking pan, smooth the top, and bake in the middle of the oven for 30 to 40 minutes, or until the cake pulls away slightly from the sides of the pan and a wooden pick inserted in the center comes out with crumbs adhering to it. Let the brownies cool completely in the pan on a rack before cutting into 2-inch bars.

BLONDIES

Yield:
30 blondies

Equipment:
baking pan, 13 by 9 by
  2 inches
hand-held electric
  mixer

Known as blondies or blonde brownies, these chewy bars are traditionally made with chocolate morsels and pecans or walnuts.

1¾ cups sifted all-purpose flour
1¼ teaspoons double-acting baking
  powder
pinch of salt
¾ teaspoon cinnamon
1¼ sticks (½ cup plus 2 tablespoons)
  unsalted butter, softened

1½ cups firmly packed light brown
  sugar
½ cup granulated sugar
2 large eggs
1½ teaspoons vanilla
1 cup (a 6-ounce package) semisweet
  chocolate morsels
¾ cup chopped pecans

Butter and flour the baking pan and preheat the oven to 350° F.

   Into a bowl sift together the flour, baking powder, salt and the cinnamon. In a large bowl with the mixer cream together the butter, brown sugar, and the granulated sugar and beat the mixture until light and fluffy. Add the eggs, one at a time, beating well after each addition, and stir in the vanilla. Add the flour mixture, stirring until the batter is blended well, and stir in the chocolate morsels and the pecans.

Pour the batter into the baking pan, smooth the top, and bake in the middle of the oven for 30 to 35 minutes, or until the cake pulls away slightly from the sides of the pan and a wooden pick inserted in the center comes out with crumbs adhering to it. Let the blondies cool completely in the pan on a rack before cutting into serving pieces.

MARBLED CHOCOLATE BUTTERSCOTCH BROWNIES

Yield:
16 brownies

Equipment:
8-inch square
baking pan

A true butterscotch flavor is obtained by melting brown sugar with butter and cooking it slightly, which gives butterscotch its characteristic nutty, buttery flavor. The use of whole-wheat flour gives this brownie a hearty flavor and helps contribute to a more healthful dessert.

FOR THE BUTTERSCOTCH BATTER

½ stick (¼ cup) unsalted butter
¾ cup firmly packed dark brown sugar
1 large egg, beaten lightly
½ cup whole-wheat flour
1 teaspoon vanilla

¼ teaspoon salt
¼ teaspoon double-acting baking powder
½ cup chopped walnuts

FOR THE CHOCOLATE BATTER

2 ounces unsweetened chocolate, chopped coarse
½ stick (¼ cup) unsalted butter
½ cup firmly packed light brown sugar
1 egg, beaten lightly

¼ cup whole-wheat flour
1 teaspoon vanilla
¼ teaspoon salt
¼ teaspoon double-acting baking powder
½ cup chopped walnuts

Make the butterscotch batter:

Make the chocolate batter:

Store in layers separated by wax paper in an airtight container.

Butter the baking pan and preheat the oven to 350° F.

In a saucepan melt the butter over moderately low heat, add the sugar, and bring the mixture to a boil, stirring, until the sugar is dissolved. Let the mixture cool. Beat in the egg, stir in the flour, vanilla, salt, and baking powder, and fold in the walnuts.

In the top of a double boiler set over hot water melt the chocolate with the butter and remove the pan from the heat. Stir in the sugar, beat in the egg, and stir in the flour, vanilla, salt, and the baking powder. Fold in the walnuts.

Pour the batters alternately in 2 batches into the baking pan and lightly swirl a knife through the mixture once to marbleize the batters. Bake in the middle of the oven for 25 to 30 minutes, or until a cake tester inserted in the center comes out clean. Transfer the dessert to a rack, let it cool, and cut it into 2-inch squares.

Photo on page 106.

BUTTERSCOTCH CRANBERRY BARS

Yield:
30 bar cookies

Equipment:
baking pan, 13 by 9 by
  2 inches

1 cup cranberries, rinsed, picked over,
  and chopped
1¾ cups plus 2 tablespoons firmly
  packed dark brown sugar
⅓ cup raisins
¼ cup dark rum
1 stick (½ cup) unsalted butter
2 large eggs, beaten lightly

1 teaspoon vanilla
1¾ cups all-purpose flour
½ teaspoon double-acting baking
  powder
½ teaspoon salt
⅔ cup chopped walnuts, toasted
  lightly

Butter the baking pan and preheat the oven to 350° F.

In a small bowl toss the cranberries with 2 tablespoons of the brown sugar and let the mixture stand for 15 minutes.

In a small saucepan combine the raisins and the rum, bring the liquid to a boil, and simmer the raisins, covered, for 5 minutes, or until they have absorbed the rum. Let cool.

In a saucepan melt the butter over moderately low heat, add the remaining 1¾ cups brown sugar, and cook the mixture, stirring, until it is just bubbly. Transfer the mixture to a heatproof bowl and let it cool for 15 minutes. Beat in the eggs and vanilla, add the flour, baking powder, and salt, and stir the batter until it is combined well. Fold in the cranberry mixture, walnuts, and raisins, turn the batter into the baking pan, spreading it evenly, and bake it in the middle of the oven for 35 to 45 minutes, or until a cake tester inserted in the center comes out clean. Let the dessert cool in the pan on a rack and cut it into bars about 2 by 1½ inches.

LINZER BARS

Yield:
32 bar cookies

Equipment:
hand-held electric mixer
8-inch square baking pan

A cookie based on the famous Viennese *Linzertorte.*

FOR THE DOUGH

1 stick (½ cup) unsalted butter, softened
½ cup firmly packed light brown sugar
¼ cup granulated sugar
⅔ cup blanched almonds (for procedure page 174), toasted lightly and ground

1 large egg, beaten lightly
1½ cups all-purpose flour
¾ teaspoon double-acting baking powder
½ teaspoon cinnamon
¼ teaspoon salt

FOR THE FILLING

¾ cup raspberry jam

1 teaspoon grated lemon rind

confectioners' sugar for sifting

Preheat the oven to 375° F.

Make the dough: In a large bowl with the mixer cream together the butter, brown sugar, and granulated sugar until the mixture is light and fluffy. Stir in the almonds and the egg.

Into a bowl sift together the flour, baking powder, cinnamon, and salt, stir the mixture into the almond mixture, and combine the dough well. Press two thirds of the dough into the baking pan. Roll out the remaining dough ⅛ inch thick between sheets of wax paper and chill it for 15 minutes, or until firm.

Make the filling: In a small bowl combine the raspberry jam and lemon rind.

With a spatula spread the filling over the dough in the baking pan. Peel off the top sheet of paper from the chilled dough, cut the dough into ½-inch strips, and arrange the strips in a lattice pattern over the jam. Bake in the middle of the oven for 30 minutes, or until golden brown. Sift the confectioners' sugar evenly over the top of the dessert, let cool, and with a serrated knife cut it into 2- by 1-inch bars.

Variation: **APRICOT LINZER BARS:** Replace the raspberry jam with ¾ cup apricot jam.

LEMON SQUARES

Yield:
16 squares

Equipment:
8-inch square pan
hand-held electric
mixer

FOR THE BASE
1 cup sifted all-purpose flour
¼ cup sifted confectioners' sugar
½ teaspoon grated lemon rind

1 stick (½ cup) cold unsalted butter,
  cut into bits

FOR THE FILLING
2 large eggs
1 cup granulated sugar
6 tablespoons fresh lemon juice

2 tablespoons all-purpose flour
½ teaspoon double-acting baking
  powder

confectioners' sugar for garnish

Preheat the oven to 375° F.

Make the base:
    In a bowl combine the flour, confectioners' sugar, and lemon rind. Cut in the butter until the mixture resembles coarse meal. Press the mixture evenly into the bottom of the ungreased baking pan. Transfer the pan to a baking sheet and bake the base in the lower third of the oven for 18 to 20 minutes, or until golden around the edges. (The base will be only partially baked at this point.)

Make the filling:
    In a large bowl with the mixer combine the eggs and the sugar. Add the lemon juice and beat the mixture for 5 minutes, or until pale and smooth. Combine the flour and baking powder. Whisk the flour mixture into the egg mixture and combine well.

Store in an airtight container, but do not refrigerate as base will become soggy.
    Pour the filling mixture over the partially baked base and continue baking the dessert on the baking sheet for 25 minutes. Sift confectioners' sugar over the dessert and let cool on a rack. Cut into 2-inch squares.

CHOCOLATE PECAN TOFFEE SQUARES

Yield:
16 squares

This bar cookie combines a crumbly shortbread base with a chewy chocolate pecan toffee topping.

Equipment:
8-inch square baking
    pan
candy thermometer

FOR THE BASE
1 cup sifted all-purpose flour   1 stick (½ cup) cold unsalted butter,
½ cup firmly packed light brown   cut into bits
    sugar

FOR THE TOPPING
1 stick (½ cup) unsalted butter   1 cup chopped pecans
2 tablespoons dark corn syrup   1 teaspoon vanilla
1 cup firmly packed light brown sugar   2 ounces semisweet chocolate, chopped
¼ cup light cream   coarse

Preheat the oven to 350° F.

Make the base:
In a bowl combine the flour and the brown sugar. Cut in the butter until the mixture resembles coarse meal. Press the mixture evenly into the bottom of the baking pan and put the baking pan on a baking sheet. Bake the base in the lower third of the oven for 35 minutes, or until golden. Let the pan cool on a rack.

Make the topping:
In a heavy saucepan melt the butter, add the dark corn syrup and the brown sugar, and bring the mixture to a boil over moderate heat, stirring with a wooden spoon. Boil the mixture, stirring occasionally, until it reaches the hard-ball stage, or the candy thermometer registers 260° F. Remove the pan from the heat and add the cream and the pecans, stirring gently. Return the pan to the heat, bring the mixture to a boil, and boil it until it reaches the soft-ball stage, or the candy thermometer registers 240° F. Remove the pan from the heat and stir in the vanilla and the chocolate, stirring until the chocolate is completely melted.

Store in layers separated by wax paper in an airtight container.
Pour the topping over the cooled base, spreading it evenly. Let the dessert cool and chill it, covered with foil, for 2 hours, or until firm. Cut into 2-inch squares.

MOLDED COOKIES

By molded cookies we mean those that are specifically shaped; not dropped or sliced, but shaped in a distinctive manner. An obvious example would be our miniature Florentines, those marvelous European creations, that actually have to be trimmed to control their glorious sugary batter. Another good example would be chocolate leaves, almond cookies actually formed into leaves with a leaf-shaped stencil. Then there are all those exceptional buttery nut cookies that are formed by hand, like the Greek Christmas classic *kourabiedes*.

Among this varied and very international collection of cookies that follows we have acknowledged our debt to the French and have included a recipe for *langues de chat*, cats' tongues, as well as one for Madeleines, which might even make Proust proud. *Langues de chat* are, of course, made with a pastry bag. Madeleines are formed in a specific mold, those lovely fluted scallop-shaped containers in which nothing else should ever be baked.

And there is another French inspiration that is a molded cookie, too—*tulipes*—those super-thin rounds made to resemble tulips by being molded in a custard cup or small glass bowl. To make a *tulipe,* as illustrated on page 153, you must work with a still-warm round. Using a spatula, transfer the cookie to a custard cup and press it carefully into the bottom of the cup. With your thumb and index finger, pinch in the opposite sides of the cookie. Repeat with the remaining sides. Let the cookie cool in the cup and when cooled it should resemble the petal shape of a tulip.

Molded cookies clearly exact some dexterity and thought. Note, for example on page 151, how to maximize the number of ladyfingers you can bake at one time by piping the batter not in equidistant rows on the baking sheet, but in staggered lines: a good solution, but one that is not immediately apparent.

Making molded cookies can be captivating, and in this very diverse and wide array is a wonderful sampling of how many cultures have cleverly met that challenge.

KOURABIEDES

Yield:
about 60 cookies

Equipment:
hand-held electric
mixer

Traditionally served in Greece at Christmas and the New Year, these rich, short, and buttery cookies are dusted heavily with confectioners' sugar and are garnished with whole cloves to recall the spices brought by the Wise Men to Bethlehem.

4 sticks (2 cups) unsalted butter,
  softened
¾ cup confectioners' sugar plus
  additional sifted for dusting

1 egg yolk
3 tablespoons Cognac
4½ cups sifted all-purpose flour
60 whole cloves

In a bowl with the mixer cream the butter until very light. Gradually add the ¾ cup sugar and continue beating until smooth and well blended. Add the egg yolk and the Cognac and beat the dough vigorously. Work in the flour, a little at a time, and beat the dough hard until smooth. Chill the dough for 1 hour, or until firm enough to handle easily.

Preheat the oven to 350° F.

With floured hands shape pieces of the dough into small balls about 1½ inches in diameter, put them on baking sheets, and stick a whole clove in the top of each. Bake the cookies in the middle of the oven for 15 minutes. Let the cookies cool on the baking sheets for several minutes and transfer them very gently to a wire rack. When the cookies are almost cool, sprinkle them generously with the sifted confectioners' sugar.

MINIATURE FLORENTINES

Yield:
about 80 cookies

Equipment:
parchment paper
2-inch round cutter
pastry brush

This classic lace cookie, studded with bits of almond and candied orange rind and brushed with melted sweet chocolate, is made even more elegant by its diminutive size.

½ cup sugar
3½ tablespoons unsalted butter
2½ tablespoons honey
2½ tablespoons heavy cream
⅔ cup sliced blanched almonds

3 tablespoons minced candied orange peel (page 168)
8 ounces dark sweet chocolate, chopped coarse

Line baking sheets with the parchment paper and preheat oven to 400° F.

In a heavy saucepan combine the sugar, butter, honey, and cream, bring the mixture to a boil over moderate heat, stirring, and boil it, stirring constantly, for 5 minutes. Stir in the almonds and the orange peel and let the mixture cool for 5 minutes. (The mixture will be very thin.)

Spoon ½ teaspoons of the mixture 2 inches apart on the baking sheets and bake the cookies in the middle of the oven for 5 minutes. Dipping the cutter into cold water each time, trim the edges of the cookies and bake the cookies for 4 to 5 minutes more, or until they are golden and bubbly. (The cookies will look runny and underdone at this point.) Let the cookies cool on the sheets for 2 minutes, or until firm enough to be transferred. Transfer them carefully with a metal spatula to racks and let them cool completely. (If the cookies become too firm to remove from the baking sheets, return them to the oven to soften for about 1 minute.)

In the top of a double boiler set over hot water melt the chocolate and remove it from the heat. Brush a thin layer of the chocolate over the smooth undersides of the cookies and let it dry. Brush a second coat of chocolate on the undersides and with the tines of a fork make a zigzag pattern lightly across it. Let the chocolate cool.

Store in layers separated by wax paper in an airtight container.

LADYFINGERS

Yield:
about thirty 3½-inch ladyfingers or about fifteen 7-inch ladyfingers

Equipment:
upright electric mixer
parchment paper
large pastry bag fitted with large plain no. 9 tip

These delicate sponge cookies are also used to line charlotte molds. Lady-fingers can be piped out to whatever length you desire, but for lining molds for charlottes or other chilled desserts, pipe them out ½ inch longer than the height of the mold.

5 egg yolks
½ cup plus 2 tablespoons granulated sugar
1 teaspoon vanilla

¾ cup all-purpose flour
7 egg whites at room temperature
¼ cup confectioners' sugar

Preheat the oven to 350° F.

In the bowl of the mixer beat the egg yolks with ½ cup of the sugar and the vanilla at number 4 speed on the mixer for 5 minutes, or until the mixture is very thick and light. Sift in the flour in 4 batches, folding in each batch before adding the next. Transfer the mixture to a large bowl. In the bowl of the mixer beat the egg whites until they hold soft peaks, sprinkle in the remaining 2 tablespoons sugar, and continue to beat the whites until they hold stiff peaks. Fold one fourth of the whites into the yolk mixture and fold in the remaining whites gently.

Put a dab of the batter on each corner of 2 baking sheets and cover the sheets with the parchment paper, pressing to make the corners adhere. Transfer the batter to the pastry bag and pipe it out in 3½-inch lengths at an angle across the length of the sheet (see illustration). Sift confectioners' sugar over the ladyfingers, then rap the sheet and tilt to remove any excess sugar. Bake the ladyfingers in the middle of the oven for 15 minutes, or until lightly colored. Remove the ladyfingers from the paper with a metal spatula, transfer them to racks, and let them cool.

Variations:

For orange- or lemon-flavored ladyfingers, add 2 teaspoons grated orange or lemon rind to the yolks. For crispy ladyfingers, sprinkle a few drops of water over the confectioners' sugar before baking the cookies. This will crystallize the sugar and result in a crunchier surface.

Piping ladyfingers at angles across length of baking sheet

CATS' TONGUES

Yield:
about 35 cookies

Equipment:
3 baking sheets
hand-held electric
   mixer
pastry bag fitted with
   ⅜-inch plain tip

These beloved long, thin, crisp butter cookies resembling a cat's tongue owe their texture to the low proportion of fat in the batter. Often referred to by their French name *langues de chat*, these cookies are the ideal accompaniment to a chilled soufflé or a frozen dessert.

½ stick (¼ cup) unsalted butter,
   softened
½ cup sugar

2 egg whites
5 tablespoons sifted cake flour (not the
   self-rising variety)

Butter heavily and flour the baking sheets and preheat the oven to 425° F.

In a bowl with the mixer cream the butter, add the sugar, and beat the mixture until light and fluffy. Add the egg whites and beat for 5 to 10 seconds, or until smooth but not frothy. (If the mixture appears curdled at this point, it is due simply to separation of the egg whites and is no cause for alarm. The batter will bind together with the addition of the flour.) Sift the cake flour over the mixture and fold it in.

Transfer the batter to the pastry bag and pipe 3-inch lengths 2 inches apart on the baking sheets, making the ends slightly wider than the middle. Rap the baking sheets on a hard surface several times to spread the batter slightly. Bake the cookies in the middle of the oven for 4 to 5 minutes, or until golden brown around the edges. Let the cookies stand on the sheets for 30 seconds, or until they are just firm enough to hold their shape, transfer them with a spatula to a rack, and let cool.

Store in layers separated by wax paper in an airtight container.

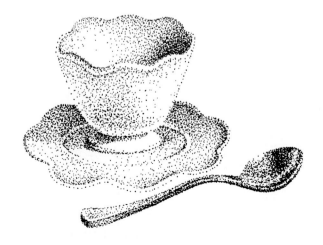

ALMOND TULIPES WITH STRAWBERRIES AND WHIPPED CREAM

Yield:
6 desserts

Equipment:
glass bowl 4 to 5 inches in diameter

This cookie is based on a very thin batter that produces a soft pliable wafer, which can be shaped while warm into fanciful forms. Here the cookie is molded in a small bowl to resemble a tulip, hence its name, almond *tulipe*.

½ stick (¼ cup) unsalted butter, softened
½ cup confectioners' sugar
¾ teaspoon almond extract
¼ cup (about 2 large) egg whites at room temperature
¼ cup all-purpose flour
⅓ cup sliced blanched almonds, toasted lightly
3 cups sliced strawberries plus 6 small strawberries, sliced, for garnish
whipped cream

Butter baking sheets and preheat the oven to 425° F.

In a bowl cream the butter, beat in the sugar, and beat until fluffy. Add the almond extract and the egg whites and beat for 5 to 10 seconds, or until smooth but not frothy. Sift the flour over the mixture and fold it in with the almonds. (The batter will be a bit lumpy.)

Spoon 1½ tablespoons of the batter onto a baking sheet and with the back of a spoon dipped in cold water spread the batter to form a 5-inch round. Continue to spoon batter onto the sheets, leaving 2 inches between each 5-inch round. Bake the cookies in the middle of the oven for 5 to 6 minutes, or until the edges are golden brown. Let the cookies stand on the baking sheets for 30 seconds, or until they are just firm enough to hold their shape, transfer them with a metal spatula to the glass bowl, and pinch in the 4 sides to make flower shapes (see illustration). If the *tulipes* become too firm to remove from the baking sheets, return them to the oven for a few seconds to soften. Let the *tulipes* cool on racks. Transfer the *tulipes* to dessert plates, divide the strawberries among them, and top each dessert with a dollop of the whipped cream and a sliced strawberry, fanned.

The tulipes can be made up to 2 days in advance. Store in an airtight container.

The *tulipes*, by virtue of their delicacy, cannot be filled in advance. Fill just before serving.

Photo on page 107.

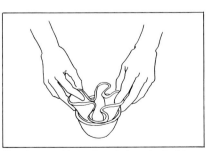

Shaping cookie wafers in bowl, pinching in sides to make *tulipe*

MADELEINES

Yield:
12 *madeleines*

Equipment:
pastry brush
12 *madeleine* molds,
  3 by 2 inches
  (available at
  specialty kitchen-
  ware stores)
hand-held electric
  mixer

The *madeleine* was forever immortalized in French literature by Marcel Proust. Through the taste of tea and one of these delicate scallop-shaped butter cakes, Proust revived, unintentionally, a childhood memory that resulted in his writing of *Remembrance of Things Past*.

about 4½ tablespoons clarified butter
  (page 164)
2 large eggs at room temperature
¼ cup granulated sugar
1 tablespoon grated orange rind

1 tablespoon fresh orange juice
½ cup all-purpose flour
¼ cup confectioners' sugar if desired
  for sifting

Preheat the oven to 375° F.

    With the pastry brush butter well the *madeleine* molds with some of the clarified butter, invert them to drain, and reserve the remaining butter.

    In a bowl with the mixer beat the eggs with the granulated sugar for 5 to 10 minutes, or until the mixture is very light and falls in a ribbon when the beater is lifted (see illustration page 10). Stir in the orange rind and orange juice. Sift the flour over the mixture, one fourth at a time, and fold it in lightly with a rubber spatula. Add the reserved clarified butter in a stream, folding it in and making sure that no butter remains at the bottom of the bowl.

    Spoon the batter into the molds, filling them two-thirds full, and arrange the molds on a baking sheet. Bake the *madeleines* in the lower third of the oven for 10 minutes, or until golden at the edges. Turn them onto a rack and let them cool. Sift the confectioners' sugar over them if desired.

    Madeleines are best the day they are made, with a cup of tea.

Variation:

ALMOND MADELEINES: In place of the orange rind and orange juice, add 1 tablespoon milk and ½ teaspoon almond extract. After folding in the sifted flour, fold in ¼ cup ground blanched almonds.

BRANDY SNAPS WITH STRAWBERRIES

Yield:
about 10 brandy snaps

Equipment:
cannoli molds
  (available at
  specialty
  kitchenware stores)
  or 1-inch-thick
  wooden dowels

FOR THE BRANDY SNAPS
½ stick (¼ cup) unsalted butter
¼ cup sugar
¼ cup unsulfured light molasses
1 teaspoon ground ginger

⅛ teaspoon salt
½ cup all-purpose flour
2 teaspoons brandy

1½ pints strawberries, hulled and
  sliced
2½ tablespoons light rum, or to taste

2½ tablespoons sugar, or to taste
whipped cream or ice cream as an
  accompaniment if desired

Make the brandy
snaps:

Butter baking sheets and preheat the oven to 325° F.

In a saucepan combine the butter, sugar, molasses, ginger, and the salt and cook the mixture over moderately low heat, stirring, until the sugar is dissolved. Remove the pan from the heat and stir in the flour and brandy.

Spoon tablespoons of the batter 6 inches apart onto the baking sheets and bake the brandy snaps in the middle of the oven for 12 to 15 minutes, or until they begin to darken. Let the brandy snaps stand on the baking sheets on a rack for 3 minutes, or until they are firm enough to roll. Wrap the brandy snaps around the *cannoli* molds or wooden dowels, let them stand until they have hardened completely, and slide them off the molds carefully. Make brandy snaps in batches with the remaining batter in the same manner, heating the batter each time if it has thickened.

The brandy snaps may
be made 1 day in
advance and kept in
an airtight container.

In a bowl toss the strawberries with the rum and the sugar, fill each brandy snap with about ¼ cup of the mixture, and serve the brandy snaps with the whipped cream or ice cream if desired.

CHOCOLATE LEAVES

Yield:
about 24 leaves

These beautiful almond-flavored cookies are formed into leaves with a traditional leaf-shaped stencil, then coated with bittersweet chocolate.

Equipment:
spice grinder
hand-held electric
  mixer
4¼-inch-long leaf-
  shaped metal stencil
  (available at
  specialty
  kitchenware stores)
  or a homemade
  heavy cardboard
  stencil

6 tablespoons sliced blanched almonds
4½ tablespoons sugar
4½ tablespoons unsalted butter,
  softened
1 large egg, beaten lightly

½ teaspoon almond extract
¾ cup sifted all-purpose flour
9 ounces bittersweet chocolate
  (preferably imported), chopped

Butter a baking sheet and preheat the oven to 300° F.

In the spice grinder grind fine, in batches, the almonds with the sugar.

In a bowl with the mixer cream the butter, add the almond and sugar mixture, and beat the mixture until it is light and fluffy. Beat in the egg, almond extract, and flour and beat the dough until it is just combined.

Lay the stencil on the baking sheet. With a metal spatula spread a heaping tablespoon of the dough over the stencil and press the dough smoothly and evenly through the stencil onto the sheet, scraping off the excess dough. Lift the stencil straight up, leaving the leaf cookie on the sheet, wipe the stencil clean, and make leaves with the remaining dough in the same manner. Bake the cookies in the middle of the oven for 10 to 15 minutes, or until the edges are just golden. Transfer them to a rack and let them cool completely.

The cookies may be
made up to 3 days in
advance and kept in a
cool place in an
airtight container.

In a bowl set over barely simmering water melt the chocolate, stirring, and transfer it to a flat plate. Working with 1 cookie at a time, lay one side flat down on the chocolate, coating it, and holding the leaf near its pointed top, lift the cookie out of the chocolate at an angle so that the chocolate drips down to the base, forming ridges like the veins of a leaf. Transfer the dipped cookies chocolate side up to a rack set on a baking sheet and chill them for 30 minutes, or until the chocolate is hardened.

ROLLED COOKIES

What this final grouping of superb cookies has in common, aside from their excellence, is that their doughs all require rolling out. These cookies will not be dropped or shaped or sliced, although some of them probably could be. Instead they will be stamped or cut out with special cutters and, as in the case of our shortbreads, those doughs will be scored.

That said, these cookies have little else in common. They are a diversified, fun lot. Among them are elegant high-style teatime cookies from Austria and rough-and-tumble gingerbread men. There are wonderful American classics like sugar cookies and a sensational almond butter cookie filled with praline buttercream.

Because we believe this set of cookies more complicated than any of those that have preceded, a few words follow on the handling of short, buttery doughs:

Always chill the dough as suggested. If you are in a hurry, hasten this process by putting the dough in the freezer for a shorter amount of time, but do not forget that it is there. What you are doing in chilling the dough is (1) relaxing the gluten in the flour, which will make for a more tender result, and (2) setting the butter to the proper consistency for rolling. If the butter becomes too hard, you will have to work the dough, which will toughen it.

■ As to the rolling-out process, flour the work surface and your cutter judiciously. Extra flour makes for a denser dough.

■ Know that the dough for some particularly short cookies, like suvaroffs and cream-filled almond butter cookies, requires being rolled between sheets of wax paper or on a pastry cloth. If you don't have a pastry cloth, substitute wax paper. In short, don't just avoid the issue entirely and proceed to roll the dough out on your board. That dough is too buttery to come up successfully.

■ In using a cookie cutter, start from the outer edge of the dough and work in. You'll have fewer scraps that way.

■ As to the rerolling of scraps, gather them into a ball of dough and roll it as gingerly as possible. At the risk of repeating ourselves, the more a dough is handled, the more it reacts negatively.

It would be inconceivable to think that you could not in this selection of cookies find the perfect cookie to fit the occasion. But who needs an occasion? A good cookie is an event in itself!

GINGERBREAD MEN

Yield:
about 50 gingerbread men

Equipment:
hand-held electric mixer
4-inch gingerbread-man cutter
pastry bag fitted with small decorative tip (optional)

2 sticks (1 cup) unsalted butter, softened
1 cup firmly packed light brown sugar
1 large egg
1 cup dark unsulfured molasses
2 tablespoons cider vinegar
5 cups all-purpose flour

2 teaspoons ground ginger
1½ teaspoons baking soda
1¼ teaspoons cinnamon
1 teaspoon ground cloves
½ teaspoon salt
1 recipe Sugar Icing (page 172) if desired

In a large bowl with the mixer cream the butter, add the sugar, and beat until fluffy. Beat in the egg, molassses, and vinegar. Into a bowl sift together the flour, ginger, baking soda, cinnamon, cloves, and the salt and stir the mixture into the butter mixture, a little at a time. (The dough will be soft.) Quarter the dough, dust it with flour, and wrap each piece in wax paper. Flatten the dough slightly and chill it for at least 3 hours or overnight.

Butter 2 baking sheets and preheat the oven to 375° F.

Roll out the dough, one piece at a time, ¼ inch thick on a floured surface. Flour the cookie cutter and cut out cookies. Transfer the cookies with a spatula to the baking sheets, arranging them 2 inches apart, and bake them in the middle of the oven for 6 to 8 minutes, or until no imprint remains when they are touched lightly with the fingertip. Transfer the cookies with the spatula to racks and let them cool. Make cookies with the dough scraps in the same manner. If desired, pipe the sugar icing decoratively on the cookies using the pastry bag. Let the cookies stand for 20 minutes, or until the icing is set.

Store in airtight containers.

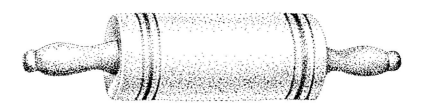

SPICE COOKIE HEARTS

Yield:
about 80 cookies

Equipment:
heart-shaped 2½-inch cutter
pastry bag fitted with very small plain tip

FOR THE COOKIES
4½ cups all-purpose flour
¼ teaspoon salt
1 teaspoon cinnamon
½ teaspoon ground ginger
½ teaspoon ground allspice

1 cup dark corn syrup
¾ cup firmly packed dark brown sugar
1 stick (½ cup) plus 2 tablespoons unsalted butter, cut into bits

FOR THE ICING
1 egg white at room temperature
1 teaspoon fresh lemon juice, or to taste

about 1 cup confectioners' sugar, sifted

Line dampened baking sheets with foil and preheat the oven to 350° F.

Make the cookies: Into a large bowl sift together the flour, salt, cinnamon, ginger, and the allspice. In a saucepan combine the corn syrup, brown sugar, and the butter and cook over moderate heat, stirring, until the butter is melted. Stir into the flour mixture and combine the mixture well to form a soft dough. Halve the dough and on the baking sheets roll out each half ⅛ inch thick. Chill the dough on the sheets for 30 minutes

Flour the cutter and with it cut out cookies, leaving at least ½ inch between the cookies. Gather the scraps and reserve them. Bake the cookies in the middle of the oven for 10 to 12 minutes, or until colored lightly, and let cool completely on the baking sheets. Make more cookies in the same manner with the reserved dough scraps.

Make the icing: In a small bowl whisk the egg white with the lemon juice until frothy. Then whisk in the confectioners' sugar, a little at a time. If the icing seems too thick, thin it with a few drops of water, or, if too thin, whisk in some additional confectioners' sugar. Transfer the icing to the pastry bag and pipe it decoratively onto the cooled cookies. Let the icing harden.

Store in airtight containers. Photo on page 108.

SUVAROFFS

Yield:
about 28 cookies

Equipment:
food processor fitted
  with steel blade
1½-inch round cutter
1-inch round cutter

An extremely short and elegant butter cookie filled with raspberry jam—a specialty in Austria.

1½ cups all-purpose flour
1½ sticks (¾ cup) cold unsalted
  butter, cut into bits

⅓ cup sugar
½ cup raspberry jam (preferably
  seedless)

In the food processor or in a bowl blend the flour and the butter until the mixture resembles coarse meal. Add the sugar and blend until a smooth dough forms. Form the dough into a ball, flatten it slightly, and chill it, wrapped in wax paper, for 1 hour.

Lightly butter baking sheets and preheat the oven to 325° F.

Roll out the dough ¼ inch thick between sheets of wax paper. Peel off the top layer of wax paper. Dipping the larger cutter in flour cut out as many rounds as possible. With the smaller cutter, floured, cut out the centers from half the rounds to form rings. Arrange the rings and the rounds carefully 1 inch apart on the baking sheets. Gather the scraps into a ball, reroll the dough, and cut out more rings and rounds in the same manner. (If the dough becomes too soft to work with, slide it with the wax paper onto a baking sheet and chill it in the freezing compartment of the refrigerator for 5 minutes, or until firm again.) Bake the cookies in the middle of the oven for 12 to 15 minutes, or until pale golden, transfer them carefully with a spatula to racks, and let them cool. Spread the flat side of each round evenly with a thin layer of the jam and top it with a ring flat side down. Fill the center of each ring with about ¼ teaspoon of the jam.

SUGAR COOKIES

Yield:
about 70 cookies

Equipment:
hand-held electric
  mixer
decorative cutters

2½ cups all-purpose flour
1 teaspoon cream of tartar
½ teaspoon baking soda
¼ teaspoon salt
¼ teaspoon freshly grated nutmeg if
  desired

2 sticks (1 cup) unsalted butter,
  softened
1 teaspoon vanilla
1¼ cups sugar
2 large eggs, beaten well
1 teaspoon grated lemon rind if desired

Into a bowl sift together the flour, cream of tartar, baking soda, salt, and nutmeg, if desired. In a bowl with the mixer cream the butter with the vanilla until light and fluffy and gradually beat in ¾ cup of the sugar to make a smooth mixture. Stir in the eggs. Add the dry ingredients gradually, combining the mixture well after each addition. Form the dough into 2 balls, dust the balls with flour, and chill them, wrapped in wax paper, for 2 hours.

Preheat the oven to 375° F.

Roll out one ball ¼ inch thick on a floured surface, cut out cookies with the cutters, and transfer the cookies with a spatula to baking sheets, arranging them 2 inches apart. Sprinkle each cookie with some of the remaining ½ cup sugar and bake in the middle of the oven for 8 to 10 minutes, or until lightly golden. Sprinkle the cookies lightly with sugar again while they are still warm. Transfer the cookies with the spatula to a rack to cool. Make cookies with the scraps and the remaining dough in the same manner.

Store in airtight
containers.

SHORTBREAD

Yield:
16 wedges

Equipment:
hand-held electric
  mixer

1½ sticks (¾ cup) unsalted butter,
  softened
½ cup sugar plus 2 tablespoons, or to
  taste, for garnish

1½ cups all-purpose flour
½ cup cornstarch

Preheat the oven to 350° F.

In a bowl with the mixer cream the butter well. Add the ½ cup sugar gradually and cream the mixture until light and fluffy. Combine the flour and the cornstarch. Add the dry mixture gradually to the creamed mixture, mixing well after each addition. Turn the dough out onto a lightly floured surface and knead it until smooth.

Divide the dough in half. Roll out each half into an 8-inch round between ¼ inch and ⅓ inch in thickness. With a large spatula put the rounds on an ungreased baking sheet and with a ruler or a sharp spatula mark each round into 8 wedges. Press the tines of a fork decoratively around the edges, sprinkle each round with 1 tablespoon of the remaining sugar, and bake in the lower third of the oven for 35 minutes, or until lightly golden and cooked through. While the shortbread is still warm cut it into wedges with a pastry wheel or large sharp knife. Transfer to racks to cool.

Store chilled in layers separated by wax paper in an airtight container.

Variation:

COCONUT SHORTBREAD: Reduce the ½ cup sugar to ¼ cup and add ½ cup sweetened flaked coconut to the dough. Knead the coconut into the dough and bake as directed above.

BROWN-SUGAR PECAN SHORTBREAD

Yield:
8 wedges

Equipment:
hand-held electric mixer

1 stick (½ cup) unsalted butter, softened
½ cup firmly packed light brown sugar
1 cup sifted all-purpose flour

¼ teaspoon salt
½ cup pecans, toasted lightly and chopped coarsely
1 tablespoon granulated sugar, or to taste, for garnish

Preheat the oven to 350° F.

In a bowl with the mixer cream the butter until light, add the brown sugar gradually, mixing well after each addition and leaving no lumps, and cream until light and fluffy. Combine the flour and salt. Add the dry ingredients gradually to the creamed mixture, mixing well after each addition. Stir the pecans into the dough.

Turn the dough out onto a lightly floured surface and knead until smooth. Roll the dough into a 9-inch round ⅓ inch thick. With a large spatula transfer the round to an ungreased baking sheet and with a ruler or sharp spatula mark it into 8 wedges. Press the tines of a fork decoratively around the edges, sprinkle the round with the granulated sugar, and bake in the lower third of the oven for 35 minutes, or until lightly golden and cooked through. While the shortbread is still warm cut it into wedges with a pastry wheel or large sharp knife. Transfer to a rack to cool.

Store chilled in layers separated by wax paper in an airtight container.

Variation:

BROWN-SUGAR WALNUT SHORTBREAD: Substitute ½ cup walnuts, toasted lightly and chopped coarsely, for the pecans.

CREAM-FILLED ALMOND BUTTER COOKIES

Yield:
about 24 sandwich
cookies

These tender and stylish almond butter cookies can be sandwiched together with almond butter cream or, for a more compelling texture, with
almond praline cream.

Equipment:
2-inch fluted round
cutter
hand-held electric
mixer

FOR THE COOKIES

1 cup finely ground blanched almonds
2 cups sifted all-purpose flour
⅔ cup granulated sugar

2 sticks (1 cup) cold unsalted butter,
cut into bits

FOR THE FILLING

2 sticks (1 cup) unsalted butter,
softened
2 teaspoons almond extract

2 cups confectioners' sugar
1 cup almond praline powder if desired
(page 167)

½ cup confectioners' sugar, sifted, for dusting

Make the cookies:

In a large bowl combine well the almonds, flour, and granulated sugar.
Cut in the butter until the mixture resembles coarse meal and turn it out
onto a lightly floured surface. Divide the dough in half, kneading each half
with the heel of your hand until smooth. Form the halves into balls, wrap
them in wax paper, and chill for 2 hours.

Preheat the oven to 350° F.

Roll one of the balls of dough ⅛ inch thick between sheets of wax paper. Peel off the top sheet of wax paper. Cut out cookies with the cutter
and transfer them with a spatula to baking sheets, arranging the cookies 2
inches apart. Bake in the middle of the oven for 13 to 15 minutes, or until
lightly golden. Let the cookies cool on the baking sheets for 1 minute and
with the spatula transfer them to a rack to cool. Make cookies with the
remaining dough in the same manner.

Make the filling:

In a bowl with the mixer cream the butter with the almond extract until
soft. Gradually add the confectioners' sugar, beating well after each addition. Continue beating the mixture for 2 minutes, until very light and
fluffy. Stir in the praline powder if desired.

**Store chilled in layers
separated by wax
paper in an airtight
container.**

When the cookies are completely cool, spread the flat sides, or bottoms, of half of them with about 1 teaspoon of the filling. Top the cookies
with the remaining halves, flat sides down, forming sandwiches. Dust the
cookies with the confectioners' sugar.

ESSENTIAL PREPARATIONS

In this final chapter of *Gourmet's Cakes, Pies, and Cookies* we have collected recipes integral to other recipes in the volume, as well as a handful of procedural instructions. The recipes make for a very varied grouping: There are syrups and icings, several chocolate preparations that serve as decorations, a marzipan recipe, and even a combination for meringue mushrooms. The procedural instructions include such basics as how to toast and skin hazelnuts, blanch almonds, and grate fresh coconut.

Some of these recipes are clearly more essential to your mastering the many aspects of dessert-making than are others. Being able to turn out a silky-smooth pastry cream is crucial to the success of a number of desserts—fruit tarts, for example, or Boston cream pie. Similarly, think of the number of recipes that rely on something as simple as perfectly whipped heavy cream. There are pies and tarts, mousse cakes, and the list could go on and on.

Alternatively, there are recipes in this chapter that are clearly less essential to other preparations elsewhere in the book, but which are interesting in their own right and will act to increase your culinary expertise. Take fondant, for example.

And there are recipes herein that would never be defined as essential except as they act as an *important* ingredient in another recipe. Among these non-essentials we would include marzipan, unless, of course, you are a dedicated cake decorator.

To review this chapter is to appreciate anew the diversity of components that comprise the glorious world of desserts.

CLARIFIED BUTTER

Yield:
about ¾ cup

Equipment:
cheesecloth
jar or crock

The butter keeps,
covered and chilled
indefinitely.

2 sticks (1 cup) unsalted butter, cut into 1-inch pieces

In a heavy saucepan melt the butter over low heat. Remove the pan from the heat, let the butter stand for 3 minutes, and skim the froth. Strain the butter through a sieve lined with a double thickness of rinsed and squeezed cheesecloth into a bowl, leaving the milky solids in the bottom of the pan. When clarified, butter loses about one fourth of its volume.

Pour the clarified butter into a jar or crock and store it, covered, in the refrigerator.

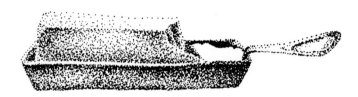

PASTRY CREAM

Yield:
1 cup

Equipment:
hand-held electric
    mixer

3 egg yolks
⅓ cup sugar
2 tablespoons cornstarch

2 tablespoons all-purpose flour
1 cup milk, scalded
1 teaspoon vanilla

In a large bowl with the mixer beat the egg yolks until combined, add the sugar, a little at a time, beating, and beat the mixture until light and lemon colored. Add the cornstarch and the flour, a little at a time, beating, and beat the mixture until smooth. Add the milk in a stream, beating, and beat the mixture until combined well. Transfer the mixture to a heavy saucepan and bring it to a boil, stirring. Simmer the mixture, stirring, for 3 minutes. The mixture will be thick and custard-like. Remove the pan from the heat and stir in the vanilla. Strain the pastry cream into a bowl and chill it, covered with a buttered round of wax paper, for 1 hour, or until chilled well.

CHOCOLATE CREAM

Crème Ganache

Yield:
about 2½ cups

8 ounces semisweet chocolate, chopped
   coarse

⅔ cup heavy cream
¼ cup orange-flavored liqueur

Equipment:
hand-held electric
  mixer

In the top of a double boiler set over hot water melt the chocolate with the heavy cream and the liqueur, stirring until smooth. Transfer the mixture to a metal bowl, let it cool, and chill it, stirring occasionally, for 30 minutes. With the mixer beat the chocolate until it just holds soft peaks.

FONDANT

Yield:
about 2 cups

2 cups sugar
¾ cup water

1 tablespoon light corn syrup

Equipment:
pastry brush
candy thermometer
moistened smooth
  surface, preferably a
  marble slab

The fondant keeps,
wrapped and chilled
indefinitely.

In a saucepan combine the sugar with the water and corn syrup and cook over low heat, washing down any sugar crystals clinging to the sides of the pan with the brush dipped in cold water until the sugar is dissolved. Increase the heat to moderately high and cook the syrup, gently swirling the pan, until the candy thermometer registers 240° F. Pour the syrup onto the moistened smooth surface and let it cool for 1 to 2 minutes. With a metal or wooden scraper work the syrup from the edges toward the center until it is white and creamy. Scrape the fondant into a ball and, when it is cool enough to handle, knead it as you would dough until smooth.

APRICOT GLAZE

Yield:
½ cup

½ cup apricot preserves, strained

1 tablespoon Cognac if desired

In a small saucepan combine the preserves and the Cognac, if desired. Bring the mixture to a boil, stirring, and simmer it, stirring, for 1 minute.

Variation:

RUM FLAVORED APRICOT GLAZE: Substitute 1 tablespoon dark rum for the Cognac.

CINNAMON SUGAR

Yield:
about 1 cup

The sugar keeps, covered tightly, indefinitely.

1 teaspoon cinnamon

1 cup granulated sugar

In a bowl combine the cinnamon with the sugar.

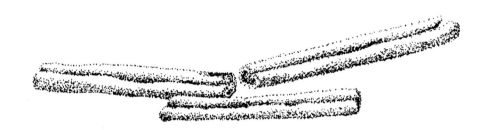

SUGAR SYRUP

Yield:
2½ cups

Equipment:
pastry brush

The syrup keeps, chilled, in a sealed jar indefinitely.

1 cup sugar

2 cups water

In a saucepan combine the sugar and water and bring the mixture to a boil, stirring and washing down any sugar crystals clinging to the sides of the pan with the brush dipped in cold water until the sugar is dissolved. Cook the syrup over moderate heat, undisturbed, for 5 minutes and let it cool.

BRANDY SYRUP

Yield:
1½ cups

½ cup sugar
1 cup water

¼ cup brandy

In a heavy saucepan dissolve the sugar in the water over moderate heat and cook the syrup for 10 minutes. Remove the pan from the heat and stir in the brandy.

ALMOND PRALINE

Yield:
about 2 cups

Equipment:
marble slab or jelly-
   roll pan
pastry brush

A wonderful dessert staple to have on hand, almond praline, ground to a powder, can also be used as a topping for ice creams, puddings, or mousses.

1½ cups sugar   *1 cup whole blanched almonds (for*
¼ cup water   *procedure page 174)*

Oil the marble slab or jelly-roll pan well.
   In a heavy saucepan bring the sugar and water to a boil over moderately high heat, stirring and washing down any sugar crystals clinging to the sides of the pan with the brush dipped in cold water until the sugar is dissolved. Cook the syrup, gently swirling the pan, until it turns a light caramel. Add the almonds and swirl the pan until the nuts are coated with the caramel and begin to make a popping sound. Boil the syrup until it is a slightly darker caramel color. Pour the praline onto the marble slab and let it cool until hard. Transfer the praline to a cutting board and chop it coarse.

The praline keeps, covered and chilled, in a glass jar indefinitely.

HAZELNUT PRALINE

Yield:
about 3 cups

Equipment:
well-oiled marble slab
   or baking sheet
pastry brush

2 cups sugar   *1½ cups hazelnuts, toasted and skins*
⅓ cup water   *removed (for procedure see page*
                                              174)

Oil the marble slab or baking sheet well.
   In a heavy saucepan bring the sugar and water to a boil over moderately high heat, stirring and washing down any sugar crystals clinging to the sides of the pan with the brush dipped in cold water until the sugar is dissolved. Cook the syrup, gently swirling the pan, until it turns a light caramel. Stir in the hazelnuts, return the syrup to a boil, and boil it until it is a slightly darker caramel. Pour the praline immediately onto the marble slab and let it cool completely. Break the praline into pieces. If praline powder is required, grind it fine in batches in a food processor fitted with the steel blade.

The praline keeps, covered and chilled, in a glass jar indefinitely.

CANDIED PECAN HALVES

Yield:
about 16 halves

Equipment:
pastry brush
candy thermometer
thin metal skewer

¼ cup water
¼ cup sugar

pinch of cream of tartar
pecan halves

In a small heavy saucepan bring the water to a boil with the sugar and the cream of tartar and cook the mixture over moderately high heat, washing down any sugar crystals clinging to the sides of the pan with the brush dipped in cold water until the syrup reaches the hard-crack stage, or the candy thermometer registers 300° F. With the skewer gently pierce each pecan half and dip it into the syrup, coating it completely. Transfer the pecans to wax paper and let them dry. Continue to candy the remaining pecans in the same mannner.

CANDIED ORANGE PEEL

Yield:
about 6 cups

Equipment:
4-quart kettle
pastry brush

The peel of citrus fruits is especially good for candying in a sugar syrup. Pink or white grapefruit or lemon peel can easily be substituted for the orange as desired. The candied peels can be served on their own, dipped in melted chocolate, or rolled in cocoa powder.

5 large navel oranges
3½ cups sugar

1¼ cups water
3 tablespoons light corn syrup

Quarter the oranges lengthwise and remove the pulp, reserving it for another use. With a spoon remove as much of the white pith as possible and cut the peel lengthwise into ½-inch strips. In the kettle cover the peel with cold water, bring the water to a boil, and simmer the peel for 10 minutes. Drain the peel, repeat the process 2 more times, and pat the peel dry with paper towels.

Line 2 jelly-roll pans with wax paper and sprinkle the paper with 1 cup of the sugar.

In the kettle combine the remaining 2½ cups sugar, the 1¼ cups water, and the corn syrup. Bring the mixture to a boil and boil it, washing down any sugar crystals clinging to the sides of the pan with the brush dipped in cold water for 20 minutes. Stir in the peel and simmer the mixture, stirring occasionally, for 15 minutes, or until the syrup is thickened. Continue to simmer the mixture, stirring constantly and being very careful not to let the syrup burn, until almost all the syrup is absorbed. Transfer the peel with tongs to the jelly-roll pans, roll each strip in the sugar to coat it well, and let the peel dry in one layer overnight.

Store in layers separated by wax paper in an airtight container in a cool, dry place. The peel keeps for up to 2 weeks.

MERINGUE MUSHROOMS

Yield:
66 confections

Equipment:
pastry brush
candy thermometer
hand-held electric
  mixer
parchment pager
pastry bag fitted with
  ⅓-inch plain tip
small star tip

Meringue mushrooms are the traditional garnish on Yule logs. See the photo of our festive Bûche de Noël on page 102.

1 cup plus 1 tablespoon sugar
¼ cup water
2 large egg whites
pinch of salt
⅛ teaspoon cream of tartar

unsweetened cocoa powder for
  sprinkling if desired
1 recipe chocolate cream (page 165)
  at room temperature

In a heavy saucepan combine the 1 cup sugar with the water and bring the mixture to a boil over low heat, washing down any sugar crystals clinging to the sides of the pan with the brush dipped in cold water until the sugar is dissolved. Boil the syrup until it reaches the soft-ball stage, or until the candy thermometer registers 240° F.

While the syrup is cooking, in a bowl with the mixer beat the egg whites with the salt until foamy. Add the cream of tartar and beat the whites for 30 seconds. Sprinkle in the remaining 1 tablespoon sugar and beat the whites until they hold stiff peaks. Add the syrup in a stream, beating, and beat the meringue for 10 minutes, or until cool.

Preheat the oven to 200° F. Line baking sheets with the parchment paper.

Fill the pastry bag fitted with the plain tip with the meringue and pipe out 66 mounds, each about 1 inch in diameter 1 inch apart onto the baking sheets. Sift a bit of the cocoa over each cap, if desired, to simulate sand. Holding the pastry bag straight up, pipe out 66 medium-wide lengths onto the baking sheets, to resemble mushroom stems. Bake the meringues in the middle of the oven for 2 hours. Remove the baking sheet from the oven and with your fingertip push in the underside of each mushroom cap. Return the meringues to the oven and bake them for 30 minutes more. Turn off the oven and let the meringues stand in the oven overnight.

Store chilled in layers
separated by wax
paper in an airtight
container.

Fill the pastry bag fitted with the star tip with the chocolate cream and pipe it into the undersides of the caps to simulate gills. Push a stem into each cap and chill the caps until the filling is firm.

MARZIPAN DECORATIONS

Equipment:
small fine-tipped paint brush

The following marzipan decorations enliven the top of Carrot Cake with Cream Cheese Frosting (page 37). Of course, marzipan can be fashioned into any shape of choice.

FOR THE MARZIPAN

one 8-ounce can almond paste, grated,
1⅔ to 2 cups confectioners' sugar,
*   sifted*

1 tablespoon vanilla
1 tablespoon lightly beaten egg white

1 tablespoon unsweetened cocoa
*   powder combined with 1 tablespoon*
*   water*
2 drops of red food coloring combined
*   with 1 tablespoon evaporated milk*
4 drops of yellow food coloring
*   combined with 2 drops of red food*
*   coloring*

3 drops of green food coloring
*   combined with 2 drops of yellow*
*   food coloring*

Make the marzipan:

In a bowl combine the almond paste, 1⅔ cups of the confectioners' sugar, the vanilla, and the egg white and knead the mixture, adding more of the confectioners' sugar if the marzipan is too sticky, until smooth.

Form one third of the marzipan into 8 small rabbits and let the rabbits dry on wax paper overnight. Chill the remaining marzipan in an airtight container. Using the brush paint the rabbits and their eyes carefully with the cocoa mixture and color their noses with the evaporated milk mixture. Knead the combined yellow and red food coloring into a small amount of the remaining marzipan and form carrots with it. Knead the combined green and yellow food coloring into a small amount of the remaining marzipan, form leaves for the carrots with some of it, and force the remaining green marzipan through a fine sieve to form grass. Transfer the grass with a small knife from the sieve to wax paper to dry for 1 hour.

CHOCOLATE CURLS

Equipment:
2 or 3 cake tins

3 ounces semisweet chocolate, chopped coarse

In the top of a double boiler set over hot water melt the chocolate, stirring until smooth. With a metal spatula spread the chocolate in a very thin layer onto the surface of the inverted cake tins. Chill the chocolate for 10 to 15 minutes, or until it loses its shine and is solid but still pliable. Removing one pan from the refrigerator at a time, put a metal spatula under an edge of the chocolate and push it firmly away from yourself along the pan so that the chocolate curls as it is pushed.

Chill the chocolate for several minutes more if it becomes too soft. Transfer the curls to a sheet of wax paper and chill them as they are made.

CHOCOLATE LEAVES

Yield:
24 leaves

3 ounces imported bittersweet chocolate, cut into bits

twenty-four 2-inch lemon leaves or other decorative nonpoisonous leaves (available at florists)

Line a jelly-roll pan with wax paper.

In the top of a double boiler set over barely simmering water melt the chocolate, stirring until smooth. With a spoon coat the back (non-shiny) side of each leaf with the chocolate, being careful not to let the chocolate drip onto the shiny side. Put the leaves, chocolate side up, on a jelly-roll pan. Prop the edges of the leaves with pieces of foil or paper towel to allow the edges to curl. Chill the leaves for 20 minutes, or until the chocolate has hardened, and, working quickly, peel off the lemon leaves. (If the chocolate gets too soft, chill the leaves for 5 minutes more, or until the chocolate has hardened.) Keep the chocolate leaves chilled until just before serving.

CHOCOLATE WHIPPED CREAM

Yield:
about 1½ cups

Equipment:
hand-held electric
  mixer

1 ounce unsweetened chocolate, chopped coarse
¾ cup well-chilled heavy cream

1 tablespoon sugar, or to taste
¼ teaspoon vanilla

In the top of a double boiler or in a large metal bowl set over barely simmering water melt the chocolate, stirring, until smooth, remove from the heat and let cool.

In a chilled bowl with the mixer beat the heavy cream with the sugar and the vanilla until it holds soft peaks. Fold the cooled melted chocolate into the whipped cream gently but thoroughly.

CHOCOLATE FUDGE ICING

Yield:
about 3½ cups

Equipment:
candy thermometer

A good fudge icing recipe is like an heirloom. It keeps being handed down, lovingly, from one generation to the next. Here is another one to add to your collection.

3 cups sugar
1 cup milk
3½ tablespoons light corn syrup

2 ounces unsweetened chocolate, cut
　into bits
½ stick (¼ cup) unsalted butter

In a heavy saucepan combine the sugar, milk, corn syrup, and the chocolate. Bring the mixture slowly to a boil and cook it over low heat until the sugar is dissolved. Cook the icing until a small drop forms a soft ball when dropped into cold water, or the candy thermometer registers 235° F. Remove the pan from the heat and beat in the butter, one tablespoon at a time. Pour the icing into a cool bowl and let it cool until just hot to the touch, or the candy thermometer registers 112° F. Beat the icing with a wooden spoon until it is of spreading consistency.

SUGAR ICING

Yield:
enough icing for
　about fifty 4-inch
　cookies

Equipment:
hand-held electric
　mixer

2 egg whites
pinch of cream of tartar
pinch of salt

2 teaspoons water
3 cups confectioners' sugar, sifted
food coloring if desired

In a large bowl with the mixer beat the egg whites with the cream of tartar, salt, and water until frothy. Beat in the sugar, a little at a time, and beat until the mixture holds stiff peaks. Beat in the food coloring if desired. Decorate baked cookies with the icing, using a spatula or a pastry bag fitted with a small decorative tip, and let the cookies stand for 20 minutes, or until the icing is set.

HARD SAUCE

Yield:
about 1 cup

Hard sauce is actually a sweetened, flavored butter and is especially good served over rich hot steamed puddings or warm fruit desserts. Despite its name, hard sauce should be served soft enough to spread.

*2 sticks (1 cup) unsalted butter,
    softened
1 cup confectioners' sugar, sifted*

*3 tablespoons amber rum
3 tablespoons brandy*

In a bowl cream together the butter and the confectioners' sugar until the mixture is fluffy and beat in the rum and brandy, one tablespoon at a time. Transfer the sauce to a serving bowl. Chill until firm but let the sauce come to room temperature before serving.

RASPBERRY SAUCE

Yield:
about 1 cup

Equipment:
food processor fitted
    with steel blade

*two 10-ounce packages frozen
    raspberries, thawed and drained
1 tablespoon lemon juice, or to taste*

*2 tablespoons superfine granulated
    sugar, or to taste*

In the food processor or in a blender purée the raspberries with the lemon juice and strain the sauce through a fine sieve into a bowl, pressing hard on the solids. Stir in the granulated sugar to taste.

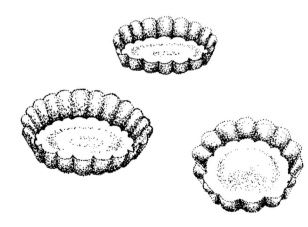

PROCEDURES

TO PEEL PEACHES

In a kettle of boiling water blanch the peaches for 30 seconds, transfer them to a bowl of ice and cold water, and slip off the skins.

TO GRATE FRESH COCONUT

Yield:
about 4 cups

Equipment:
food processor fitted
  with steel blade

1 large coconut without any cracks and containing liquid

Preheat the oven to 400° F.

Pierce the eyes of the coconut with an ice pick or a skewer, drain the liquid, and reserve it for another use. Bake the coconut for 15 minutes. Break it with a hammer and remove the flesh from the shell, levering it out carefully with the point of a strong knife. Peel off the brown membrane with a vegetable peeler and cut the coconut meat into small pieces. Grind the pieces a few at a time in the food processor or in a blender. (Or grate the meat on the fine side of a grater.)

TO BLANCH ALMONDS

Into a large saucepan of boiling water drop the almonds. Boil them for 1 minute, or until the skins wrinkle, and drain them in a colander. Refresh the almonds under cold water, slip off the skins by squeezing the almonds between two fingers, and pat the almonds dry. Let the almonds stand in one layer on a baking sheet for 2 hours, or until they are completely dry. Do not dry the almonds in the oven.

TO TOAST AND SKIN HAZELNUTS (OR FILBERTS)

Preheat the oven to 350° F.

Toast the hazelnuts in one layer in a jelly-roll pan for 10 to 15 minutes, or until they are colored lightly and the skins blister. Wrap the nuts in a dish towel and let them steam for 1 minute. Rub the nuts in the towel to remove the skins and let them cool. Note that some of the hazelnuts will not be completely skinned; they can be used nonetheless.

RECIPE TITLE INDEX

Italic numbers refer to color photographs.

Gourmet's Cakes, Pies, and Cookies has been excerpted from *Gourmet's Best Desserts*. For more information, write to: Gourmet Books, P.O. Box 10850, Dept. 245118, Des Moines, Iowa 50336.